EXPERIENCE AND CERTAINTY

ÆR

American Academy of Religion
Studies in Religion

Editors
Charley Hardwick
James O. Duke

Number 50
EXPERIENCE AND CERTAINTY
William Ernest Hocking and Philosophical Mysticism

by
Margaret Lewis Furse

EXPERIENCE AND CERTAINTY
William Ernest Hocking and
Philosophical Mysticism

by
Margaret Lewis Furse

Scholars Press
Atlanta, Georgia

EXPERIENCE AND CERTAINTY
William Ernest Hocking and Philosophical Mysticism

by
Margaret Lewis Furse

Library of Congress Cataloging-in-Publication Data

Furse, Margaret Lewis.
  Experience and certainty

  (Studies in religion / American Academy of Religion ;
no. 50)
  Bibliography: p.
  1. Hocking, William Ernest, 1873-1966—Contributions
in the philosophy of mysticism. 2. James, William,
1842-1910—Contributions in philosophy of mysticism.
3. Royce, Josiah, 1855-1916—Contributions in philosophy
of mysticism. 4. Mysticism—History—20th century.
I. Title II. Series: Studies in religion (American
Academy of Religion) ; no. 50.

B945.H64f87 1987   191   87-16545
ISBN 1-55540-164-3 (alk. paper)
ISBN 1-55540-165-1 (pbk. : alk. paper)

Printed in the United States of America
on acid-free paper

To
A. H. F.
for
Happy Partnership

CONTENTS

PREFACE

In this book I have tried to attend to several aims at once. One aim, which I suppose is with me always, is to aspire to the virtues of brevity and clarity. But in the process of writing, I began to see those two virtues coming into conflict. At first, I intended to be so brief in my treatment of James and Royce that I would mention them and their bearing on Hocking just in passing. I soon found, however, that to mention James or Royce in passing is to pass off the northern lights with a comment on nice weather. In order to be clear about James, and especially to be clear about Royce who, as even James complained, does not always aid the task, I have extended my treatment of them somewhat beyond my original intention. The book is about Hocking on mysticism and not about all three equally; however, because of the slight shift in emphasis, the reader will experience some delay after Hocking is introduced before the story of Hocking begins again in earnest. The exposition of James and Royce that fills the interval is both relevant and important to an understanding of Hocking and, it is to be hoped, worthwhile in itself.

The James-Royce interval required some small compromise with another of my aims, a pedagogical one. I would like to address, among others, the nontechnical reader who can use an introduction to mysticism as a philosophical view and the reader who can use an introduction to Hocking's philosophy in general by means of his view of mysticism. For such readers some of the material that precedes Hocking—Royce's distinction between the internal and external meaning of an idea, for example—might come as an unwelcome complication. For an introduction to mysticism, Hocking's introduction in *Types of Philosophy* (summarized in Chapter 4) is a good place to start. Some readers, then, may choose to follow the sequence that best suits their interests. Chapters concerned exclusively with Hocking could be read first, and those on James and Royce could be deferred. If the reader is good enough to be flexible and forgiving, perhaps some awkwardness can be smoothed over and the reader's own interest better served. I think there would be no serious loss of continuity in adopting that plan.

Another of my aims has been expository. By that I simply mean that I have tried to give a good, brief, accurate account of "what was said" by Hocking and also by James and Royce. I have been mainly concerned, of course, with what each has said on mysticism. As everyone would agree, the better way to know what was said by the three is to read them directly. And a main purpose has been to give the reader some assistance in doing just that. I had, in fact, originally planned the chapters on Hocking as an introduction to an anthology of Hocking on mysticism.[1]

My expository aim requires in turn that I keep my own critical voice still—or at least identifiable as my own and not that of the writers I am expositing—*while* I am expositing. I believe I have managed to do so especially in the case of Hocking. Chapters 4 and 5 are an exposition of the relevant chapters on mysticism in Hocking's *Types of Philosophy* and a synopsis of his argument in *The Meaning of God in Human Experience*. I have largely reserved criticism of Hocking for Chapter 6. In the chapter on James, I have tried faithfully to present "what was said" by James in his *Varieties of Religious Experience*. I have kept very close to James's order of presentation and to his own language in *Varieties*. In fact, when it comes to William James, it is difficult to resist keeping close to his language. When he says (in "The Will to Believe") that the failure to risk belief is to be shut up in "snarling logicality" or says (in *Varieties*) that the act of perception has in it "something that glimmers and twinkles . . . for which reflection comes too late," it is really impossible not to quote him. In contrast to James, I have found Royce more difficult to present clearly if one keeps slavishly to his own language and order of presentation. Some of his examples make his point much more clearly than others, and I have been selective in presenting them. I believe that I have faithfully represented rather than mirrored his view in the relevant chapters of *The World and the Individual*. I have, however, tried to be especially careful to follow "what was said" by him in his essay on the medieval mystic Meister Eckhart. The chapters on Royce and James do include some of my own critical comments and sizings up; I think they are identifiable as such. Also, the notes often contain a more extensive clarifying quotation or critical comment than the text.

I have found that I could not attend to my expository and pedagogical aims and, at the same time, do full justice to the philosophical relationship among Hocking, James, and Royce. Largely I have had simply to set down the three in a line and content myself with pointing out, here and there, resemblances and divergences. The story of James and Royce has been told in many excellent studies, and I can add nothing to them. To say in any greater detail than I do just how Hocking relates to James and Royce in epistemology and metaphysics would certainly put the discussion on a

[1]The anthology would have included chapters recommended by Hocking. Hocking's advice on what to read from his work on the subject of mysticism is given in the bibliography of *Types of Philosophy*, 3d ed. (New York: Charles Scribner's Sons, 1959), p. 328. In addition to Chaps. 33, 34, 35, and 36 in *Types of Philosophy*, Hocking recommends the following in *The Meaning of God in Human Experience*: Part 5, "Worship and the Mystics," and Part 6, "The Fruits of Religion," especially Chap. 28, "The Principles of Alternation," which he recommends following with Chap. 26, "The Mystic's Preparation," Chap. 24, "Thought and Worship," and Chap. 32, "The Prophetic Consciousness."

technical plane, leave the expository aim unfulfilled, and turn the book into one about all three—Royce, James, and Hocking. A project of that kind would be a good one, but it is not the book I have had in mind.

Another worthwhile project that I have obviously not had in mind here either is to address fully the historian's interest in having Hocking placed within the elaborate context of American culture. Hocking would indeed be an excellent subject for a full "life and thought" treatment, and I hope that someone will produce such a work. This book with its more modest set of aims is, of course, not such a work.

To the reader whose interest is philosophically more technical, I can say that I do not offer any new discoveries or any altogether new interpretations, but a new presentation and focus: What is mysticism? And what role does it play in the philosophical idealism of William Ernest Hocking and, incidentally, in the philosophy of his mentors, William James and Josiah Royce? What are we to think of the mystics' (and of Hocking's) assertion that certainty lies within human experience? What is the religious role for doubt?

I hope that this book might serve in a small way to make Hocking accessible to a wider and more popular audience than his work has recently enjoyed. Hocking, I believe, deserves to be rediscovered and read by students of American philosophy and American culture and by students of theology and philosophy of religion. He is a clear interpreter of mysticism, and he is an excellent example of American philosophical idealism. He writes elegant philosophical prose in the formal style of his day. Some of his insights have a timeless value, and they are useful, as he intended the philosopher's work to be, for anyone with a vocation to live well and generously and wisely, and in community with others, which implies, as Hocking believed, community with an Other.

Margaret Lewis Furse
Austin, Texas

ACKNOWLEDGMENTS

I am glad to have this opportunity to thank friends at the University of Texas and elsewhere for advice and other assistance in the preparation of this manuscript.

At the University of Texas, both Louis Mackey of the Department of Philosophy and Jeffrey Meikle of the Program in American Studies generously set aside their own work at a busy time to give my manuscript a very helpful critical reading.

For promptness, judgment, and tactful criticism, I thank James O. Duke of the Pacific School of Religion and Charley D. Hardwick of the American University. They are the editors of the American Academy of Religion series, *Studies in Religion*, of which this book now becomes a part.

I am especially glad to have this chance to thank Genene Oestrick, who has helped me greatly in the preparation of this manuscript and in countless other ways over a period of several years.

Because I have just concluded more than a decade of teaching at the University of Texas at Austin, it is only with difficulty that I suppress the impulse to name here "all those" students and colleagues who have made that experience the delight that it certainly has been. I must, however, name and warmly thank the innovative American Studies Program which has, over the years, encouraged me in developing new courses in religious studies and ethics. Also, my gratitude is too keenly felt not to express it to members of the Religious Studies Committee of the College of Liberal Arts which, for a number of years, I served as chairman. In that capacity I had many occasions to appreciate the helpfulness and friendship of Deans Robert D. King, Joseph M. Horn, and the wonderful members of their staff.

CHAPTER 1
HOCKING'S PHILOSOPHICAL MYSTICISM

William Ernest Hocking (1873–1966) was one of America's most distinguished and influential philosophers. Like his teacher and colleague Josiah Royce, he was a representative of philosophical idealism, but Hocking's idealism, unlike that of Royce, was a religious empiricism, an intuitionism or mysticism. Hocking had a long career in the philosophy department at Harvard and influenced many professional philosophers, among them the American process philosopher Charles Hartshorne and the French Catholic existentialist Gabriel Marcel. Charles Hartshorne has said that Hocking gave him his first real grounding in the discipline of philosophy. He remembers Hocking at Harvard as a handsome, very impressive presence, always able to command the attention of his audience. Gabriel Marcel credited Hocking with showing him how to overcome solipsism through an intuited sense of another's presence.

For several decades, from about 1929 until the late 1950s, countless undergraduates had their introduction to philosophy through Hocking's textbooks. His widely used text *Types of Philosophy* was first published in 1929, and continued in print in its third edition of 1959. Another text, and one of the first to appear in the post–World War II period, was *Preface to Philosophy* (1947), to which Hocking contributed along with Brand Blanshard, Charles William Hendel, and John Herman Randall, Jr.

Hocking's constructive philosophical writing ranged over such a broad selection of subjects that his work, as a whole, is difficult to characterize. One writer who has very successfully done so is Leroy S. Rouner with his good critical introduction *Within Human Experience: The Philosophy of William Ernest Hocking* (1969). Rouner has also edited a collection of critical essays as a *Festschrift* for Hocking called *Philosophy, Religion, and the Coming World Civilization: Essays in Honor of William Ernest Hocking* (1966). That volume includes contributions by Gabriel Marcel, Charles Hartshorne, Henry Nelson Wieman, Henry Pitney Van Dusen, F. S. C. Northrop, Charles Moore, Crane Brinton, Neils Ferre, John E. Smith, Andrew J. Reck, Walter Stace, and others. Another very helpful general treatment of Hocking with an excellent bibliography is that of A. R. Luther, *Existence as Dialectical Tension* (1968).

Hocking wrote on law, politics, and international affairs; on human nature (in *Human Nature and Its Remaking*, 1918); and even on freedom of the press (in *Freedom of the Press: A Framework of Principles*, 1947). And, at a time when Neo-orthodox theologians like Karl Barth and Emil Brunner were stressing Christian uniqueness, Hocking, who was distinctly cosmopolitan in his Christianity, provided an inclusive framework for world religions in two books, *Living Religions and a World Faith* (1940) and *The Coming World Civilization* (1956). Even though in a long life, Hocking devoted himself to a great many subjects, his chief subject always remained philosophy of religion. And, as we shall see, one of the keys to his philosophy of religion was the role he gave to mysticism.

Hocking's first and definitive book on philosophy of religion was *The Meaning of God in Human Experience*. That work, first published in 1912, was republished by the Yale University Press in 1963 when Hocking was ninety. In his 1963 preface he said that a main problem of modern philosophy had been how to overcome solipsism. Is the self in an isolated state, walled in behind sensory stimuli, unable to reach over to any substance behind the sensory stimuli, unable even to know the experience of another self, and, therefore, unable to experience an absolute self, God?

Hocking's main effort in *The Meaning of God in Human Experience* is to answer no to these questions. In that work he suggests that one ought not to begin with natural objects as if they had some prior, preferred, and utterly independent standing in reality: objects in nature have their objectivity credited to them because they are the sharable experience of kindred selves. Other selves can indeed be known and their experiences shared, even immediately entered into, by the knowing self. And this is true, Hocking argues, because the ground of all reality is social being, Absolute Self. And this Absolute Self or God is immediately and permanently known to finite selves sharing, as they do, the social nature of the Absolute Self. The prior, certain, and immediately experienced reality from which all other convictions are derived is God.

Hocking said that this, his earliest book, was in a sense autobiographical. The convictions elaborated in it represented a confidence he himself had attained in his own personal reflections. One of the most vivid autobiographical descriptions of the direct experience of overcoming solipsistic social isolation is given as an example in *The Meaning of God in Human Experience* (Hocking's "comrade" is his wife Agnes):

> I have sometimes sat looking at a comrade, speculating on this mysterious isolation of self from self. Why are we so made that I gaze and see of thee only thy Wall, and never Thee? This Wall of thee is but a movable part of the Wall of my world; and I also am a Wall to thee; we look out at one another from behind masks. How would it seem if my mind could but once be *within* thine; and we could meet and without barrier be with each other? And then it has fallen upon me like a shock—

as when one thinking himself alone has felt a presence—But I
am in thy soul. These things round me are in thy experience.
They are thy own; when I touch them and move them I change
thee. When I look on them I see what thou seest; when I listen
I hear what thou hearest, I am in the great Room of thy soul;
and I experience thy very experience. . . .[1]

[1] William Ernest Hocking, *The Meaning of God in Human Experience* (New Haven: Yale
University Press, 1912), pp. 265–66. Hocking thinks that knowledge of other selves is a problem
if one takes knowledge of natural objects as the norm. One is then unable to know the self
because the knowing of any object is explained "by a relation between object and subject, in
which the object presumably produces some effect on the subject, and we find naturally enough
that anything which is intrinsically subject cannot become an object." Ibid., p. 251. Hocking
interprets nature and body as the "metaphor" of the other self and also as the "literal edge" of the
Other Spirit shimmering through its physical encasements." Ibid., p. 265. The three areas in
which this "literal edge" are discerned are the shared experience of time, of space, and of
continuity within change, i.e., personal history and identity.

Certainly it is Hocking's own vivid personal experience of discerning the "literal edge" of the
other that is represented in the described scene with "a comrade." Hocking says, "I confess that
this extraordinary device by which Other Mind presents itself in the guise of body in the midst
of Nature seems to me each time I think of it more wonderful than before. The inseparable
union of two things so disparate as social experience and experience of Nature seem to be: is
there not a perpetual amazement in this?" Ibid.

Immediate experience of other minds is in a sense the key to Hocking's thought because God
is the social reality or context which makes that knowledge possible: "My current social
experience, the finding of any fellow finite mind is an application of my prior idea of an Other; in
a sense, *an application* of my idea of God. *It is through the knowledge of God that I am able to
know men; not first through the knowledge of men that I am able to know or imagine God.*"
Hocking's emphasis. Ibid., pp. 297–98.

If Hocking had had Buber's language of "I-Thou" and the "Eternal Thou" and such a phrase as
"In the beginning is relation," one wonders whether he would have explained himself in these
terms. (Buber's *I-Thou* appeared in German in 1923 and in English in 1937.) In the few hints
that we have, his answer is equivocal. In 1956, Hocking wrote a preface to the English
translation of Gabriel Marcel's *Royce's Metaphysics*. In it he recalls submitting to his teacher,
Josiah Royce, an essay on the problem of other minds. We quote Hocking's memory of the
session with Royce in the year 1903–1904, the last year of Hocking's graduate study at Harvard:

> I ventured to differ from one of his central doctrines, namely that we have
> no direct knowledge either of our own minds or of other minds. For, as he
> held, selves are individuals; and individuals are beings such that, for each one,
> there can be in the whole universe no other precisely like it: this is what we
> mean by our individual attachments. Such uniqueness can be no matter of
> empirical knowledge: it is rather a matter of will: "it is thus that the mother
> says, There shall be no child like my child" (World and Individual, 458–460),
> *ergo* no possible substitution, no recompense for loss. In this particular essay,
> I reported an experience in which as I read it, I was directly aware of another
> mind and my own as co-knowers of a bit of the physical world, a "Thou" and an
> "I" as co-knowers of an "It." So far as feeling was involved, that *feeling was
> cognitive*, not simply an I-will: we must extend the conception of empirical
> knowledge, and so admit an element of realism within the ideal totality. I was
> expecting a radical criticism from my revered professor. Instead, when Royce
> handed my essay back, he pointed out the dissenting passage with the

In *The Meaning of God in Human Experience,* one of Hocking's aims is to be both an idealist and an empiricist. He developed his kind of idealism by appropriating mysticism as a philosophical resource. Were not mystics people who assumed an idealistic monism? And were they not also, in some inclusive sense of the word, empiricists (epistemological realists) who reported their immediate experience of the Absolute One? Hocking thought that mystical experience (defined broadly as the intuition and worship of the Absolute or God) was not an esoteric experience and was not an experience confined to religious specialists like the classic mystics of history. Mystical experience was normal in human nature and open to all religiously sensitive

comment, "This is your insight: you must adhere to that!" Without assenting to my view, he had given me his blessing for its development.

—Gabriel Marcel, *Royce's Metaphysics,* trans. Virginia and Gordon Ringer (Westport: Greenwood Press, 1975), pp. vii–viii.

In 1964, Hocking was one of a number of philosophers who sat down with Martin Buber and put questions to him in a seminar setting. Hocking's questioning shows that he preferred a greater role for reasoning ("dialectic") than Buber's "dialogical" approach seemed to Hocking to allow.

Hocking identifies the "locus" of his question to Buber this way: "The real as given in experience rather than pure reason; immediacy vs. concept; prophet vs. philosopher; yet dialectic as the *conscience* of realization."

He goes on: "Although we properly distinguish realization of the Real, as in the immediate experience of togetherness in 'meeting,' from any process of conceptual thought or any result thereof, may not conceptual reasoning—let us say dialectic—be present in that realization, as it were in solution? And may not that dialectic be a potent aid in giving currency to the experience itself?"

It is true, Hocking agrees, that the kind of truth involved in I-Thou encounter is one "discovered" and not proved. Dialectic alone cannot bring it about. Yet dialectic may be "the midwife of vision."

Speaking as I must from my own experience, I testify that when this "realization" arrived—a very definite experience—it followed a period of wrestling and anxiety due to perplexities over internal contradictions of thought in which the subjective necessities stemming from Descartes and Kant contended with objective necessities I could not banish—the Real must be in some sense *other;* and the resolution through what appeared to be a dialectical discernment was definitely relevant to the joy of realization: dialectic was the midwife of vision.

Hocking suggests that the ghost of the philosopher can live within the soul of the prophet and can sanction the prophet's appeal. "Sometimes the two speak with one voice." If this is true, then could not "system . . . be defended as not inconsistent with the life of realization and relation, and further, as its integrity, its inner coherence?" Could systematic thought be the "conscience" of vision and encounter?

Buber replied that something other than dialectic calls forth "the decisive turning" that marks I-Thou encounter. Yet the consequence of "a direct dialogical reality," the discussion of it and communication of it is admittedly dialectical. Sydney and Beatrice Rome (eds.), *Philosophical Interrogations* (New York: Holt, Rinehart and Winston, 1964), pp. 45–47.

persons. So one of Hocking's methodological aims in *The Meaning of God in Human Experience* was to be an absolute idealist like Royce. But Hocking intended to be an empiricist, too. In the empiricism he espoused, however, he held a much larger and more dynamic view of what constituted experience than had prevailed in the atomistic British empiricism of Locke, Berkeley, and Hume. In Hocking's day William James was mainly responsible for articulating this enlarged view of experience in general and of religious experience in particular.

Another of Hocking's aims, and one not easy to reconcile with the first, was to proceed in some ways like James, the pragmatist. Hocking begins *The Meaning of God in Human Experience* with the thought that idealism needs some correction by means of pragmatism. Pragmatism was right to ask about actual effects. What difference did the Absolute make in actual experience here and now? Idealism by itself, without a pragmatic interest in results, was too remote. It seemed to Hocking to offer only a "religion-in-general."

When Hocking was a young man, James's ideas had been to him like a breath of fresh air. Hocking, born in Cleveland, Ohio on August 10, 1873, was the son of a physician, whose family was Methodist and devout. Hocking developed an early interest in science and began reading his father's medical books—a practice frowned on by his parents. At the age of fifteen, when he came across Herbert Spencer's *First Principles* and read it carefully, he suffered a complete disillusionment, an immediate conversion to Spencer's materialism. Spencer's argument seemed then too plausible to be answered. "Thoroughly against my will," he wrote, "and with a sense of unmeasured inner tragedy, Spencer convinced me. . . . Spencer had the truth—such modest truth as was to be had. He had written blank mystery over the original splendour of the uncharted world. His view demanded unqualified resignation to the outlook of animal death—to me a sweeping desolation."[2]

James is the person Hocking credits with his "release" from Spencer's paralyzing thrall. Hocking describes the day that he was browsing through the shelves of the public library and happened to run across James's new book *The Principles of Psychology* (1890). The impact of this book was immediate. It "irrigated certain tracts that had become desert. I began to regain confidence that the mystic's sense of the universe is in substance a true sense. . . ."[3] Hocking went to study at Harvard, arriving, it so happened, just when James was away in Edinburgh delivering his Gifford Lectures, *Varieties of Religious Experience*. When James returned to present those lectures at Harvard, Hocking says that he went to him with the "enthusiasm of deferred hope." James "read his marvelous manuscript on

[2] William Ernest Hocking, "Some Second Principles," in George P. Adams and William Pepperell Montague (eds.), *Contemporary American Philosophy*, Vol. 1, *Personal Statements* (New York: Russell & Russell, Inc., 1962, first published 1930), p. 387.
[3] Ibid., p. 388.

religious experience. The stuff of that work was grist for my mill; James was indeed a liberator, and in his presence life was in the saddle."[4]

At the turn of the century, James had been instrumental in making the subject of mysticism relevant for a generation of scholars. Hocking's personal disposition and philosophical idealism disposed him to follow James in giving mystical experience a prominent role in his philosophy of religion. Hocking's work on mysticism not only provides a good introduction to his thought, but should be of general interest to students of religion for two other reasons.

First, everyone recognizes that the study of religion inevitably raises questions about religious experience: What is it? What is its philosophical significance? Where is it? Inside the self? Between the self and its object? Between self and Self? Does it deliver any transcendent reality to the experiencing self?

Questions like these raise the possibility of a role for mysticism and mystical experience, and Hocking develops his analysis of mysticism with great assurance that experiential certainty of God is an obtainable philosophical aim. Philosophy, he held, must aim at real knowledge, at certainty. "I believe," he said, "in a mystical realism . . . the only tenable sort of realism." The only empirical, experimental attitude is the mystic's attitude. Only with the attitude of the mystic is anyone willing to revise assumptions. Mystics directly apprehend (for a limited time) the absolute, which enables them to see any given belief as tentative, relative, and revisable. "The true experimental spirit," he says, "is that of the mystic, who regards every fixed habit as tentative, and every conceptual standard as provisional, not because there is nothing absolute, but because there is [an absolute]." Mystics are those who can renew from time to time their perception of "that absolute real and good" and in so doing can prepare themselves "for those fresh contacts with reality in social and natural experience" that encourage a revision of assumed axioms and prejudice.[5]

Hocking thinks that any creditable philosophical view, and especially his own philosophical idealism, should be able to show its everyday relevance to life as people actually live it. Experience is the arena in which a philosophical view should prove itself. It is true, however (and we will have more to say about this as this study unfolds), that Hocking interpreted experience as a very large, inclusive, and imperfectly demarcated arena. He even held "that a theory is false if it is not interesting." If a proposition "falls so dully as to excite no enthusiasm," it has not reached "the level of truth."[6] For Hocking, then, the question of religious experience arises whenever the deepest

[4]Ibid., p. 389.
[5]William Ernest Hocking, *Types of Philosophy*, 3d ed. (New York: Charles Scribner's Sons, 1959), p. 318.
[6]Hocking, *The Meaning of God in Human Experience*, p. xiii.

significance of any experience arises, and when it does arise, some study of mysticism becomes necessary and exceedingly valuable.

Another reason to study Hocking on mysticism is that he happens to provide one of the clearest definitions and discussions of mysticism found in modern studies of it. Hocking's discussion of mysticism in *Types of Philosophy* is an excellent place to begin for anyone who would like to have an introduction to mysticism regarded both as one possible philosophical world view and as the common religious attitude of all human beings sensitive to the deeper significance of experienced facts.

When we read the preface and text of Hocking's *The Meaning of God in Human Experience*, it is obvious that he writes with an eye to his mentors, William James and Josiah Royce. He absorbs a good deal from both, but he is also critical of both. In this study it will not be possible to draw what would be the very complicated map of the relationship among the three. We can, however, as an addition to our main interest in Hocking and mysticism, simply put into view what James and Royce had to say of mysticism.

We will find Royce much more confident of the role of reasoning in religion than was James. The Absolute is logically entailed, Royce insists, once anyone asserts that there is truth and error. One cannot assert that a counterposition is in error without invoking the Absolute Consciousness within which truth and error find their contrast.

James doubts the validity of this sort of argument (or of scholastic arguments, for that matter). He does not think that anyone really decides to believe on grounds of logical proof—unless the feeling and disposition to act in behalf of belief are already in place. Hocking is sympathetic with James's position and its implied criticism of a Roycian idealism. Even if the idealistic arguments had undeniable logical force, do they really culminate, asks Hocking, in the God of religion who can be worshipped? Hocking holds that many critics of such arguments "do not find the Absolute of idealism identical with the God of religion: they cannot worship the Absolute. And they do not find that religion consists in our human knowledge of this absolute Knower: *Denken*, they think, *ist nicht Gottesdienst*."[7] In this criticism, Hocking has Royce in mind.

But Hocking finds James far too quick to let go of certainty and knowledge and to settle only for hypothesis. James's "will to believe" is all right as a principle of action, but it does not yield what we must have, knowledge. No one who adopts hypothesis of belief as a working theory simply winks at "the difference between postulate and knowledge."[8]

If James's pragmatism, then, simply resorts to a religion of feeling (as Hocking thinks that it does), and gives up certainty, it has taken a wrong turn in its criticism of idealism. One of the pragmatic needs in religion is to have

[7] Ibid., p. vi.
[8] Ibid., p. xvi.

knowledge and to have certainty. Hocking finds the best critic of idealism to be not pragmatism but mysticism. Mysticism has its absolute and it "finds its metaphysic in experience." Mysticism is a form of idealism, then, that "is no stranger to worship."[9]

In the next two chapters we sketch the context in which Hocking wrote about mysticism and review briefly the respective positions of his distinguished teachers, William James and Josiah Royce.

---

[9] Ibid., p. xviii.

CHAPTER 2

JAMES AND THE MODERN STUDY OF MYSTICISM

Because William James was ill, his Gifford Lectures had to be postponed and, with an uncharacteristic trace of bitterness, Mrs. James lamented to her brother-in-law, Henry James, Jr., that Royce would now take his place: "Royce!! *He* will not refuse, but over he will go with his Infinite under his arm, and he will not even do honour to William's recommendation."[1] Royce did take his Infinite over to the University of Aberdeen in his Gifford Lectures of 1899 and 1900, *The World and the Individual*. James's postponed lectures, delivered in Edinburgh in 1901, were *Varieties of Religious Experience* (published in 1902).

Mrs. James's moment of disappointment at having Royce's lectures replace her husband's was in a way a sign of the times. Theirs was a day when competing philosophies had become, as William James expressed it, "so many religions, ways of fronting life, and worth fighting for." In 1900, James told George Herbert Palmer, chairman of the philosophy department at Harvard, that the proper philosophical climate to aim for there "would be an open conflict of rivalry of diverse systems." If we at Harvard "devoted ourselves exclusively to belaboring each other," then "the world might ring with the struggle."[2]

For James, Royce, Hocking, and their contemporaries, there was passion, tension, and even solemn religiosity in the constructive work of philosophy. Possibly it was a new *separation* of philosophy from theology that reinvested philosophy with a kind of religious fervor. Earlier, in 1865, George Herbert Palmer tells us that it was hardly possible for an American student to study philosophy at all outside a theological seminary. He himself had had to get his philosophy at Andover Seminary.[3] Even John Dewey, in his graduate student days, wondered where a nontheologian philosopher

---

[1] Quoted in Gay Wilson Allen, *William James: A Biography* (New York: Viking Press, 1967), p. 387. The letter is dated April 23, 1897.

[2] Quoted in Allen, *William James*, p. 414. The letter is dated April 2, 1900.

[3] George P. Adams and William Pepperell Montague (eds.), *Contemporary American Philosophy*, Vol. 1, *Personal Statements* (New York: Russell & Russell, Inc., 1962, first published 1930), p. 23.

might find employment. But by about 1900, philosophy had assumed a more independent role and possibly more seemed now to be put at risk by adopting one philosophical system as opposed to another. In doing so one accepted or rejected a whole belief system rather than an auxiliary to received religious doctrine. Whether one's intellectual loyalty was to Idealism, Naturalism, Pragmatism, or some other philosophical school was a question of animated discussion and letterwriting. Sometimes the tone of James's, Hocking's, and Royce's letters almost suggests an intellectual denominationalism.

When philosophy did begin to loosen itself from an implied theological alliance, it could then scrutinize religion from a friendly distance. The new scrutiny was not necessarily carried on in a hostile spirit, but in a lively, liberal, critical spirit that could very well end in warm appreciation. This was a spirit that took religion seriously but which could, if it chose, stand free of churchly identification. A common assumption, shared by James, Royce, and Hocking and well expressed by Royce's book title, *The Religious Aspect of Philosophy* (1885), was that the philosopher's motive, at bottom, was religious. The philosopher's work was charged with the solemnity of a high calling. And the results of it should prove their worth by the edification of character. This approach was eminently the philosophical stance of Hocking. And dating from about the time of James's lectures, it was the usual style in which studies of mysticism were undertaken by a group of world scholars, among whom Hocking was a prominent younger member.

Some Modern Interpreters of Mysticism

Many of these scholars looked to a mystical type of religion as a way of avoiding a conflict between science or historical criticism on the one hand and dogmatic theology on the other. In the early twentieth century, studies of mysticism and a *modernist* impulse were allied. Thus the subject of mysticism was not usually regarded as an irrational type of religiosity, but as a deeper or wider kind of rationality.[4]

Among the early twentieth century interpreters of mysticism in England we should name Evelyn Underhill, William Ralph Inge, and Friedrich von Hügel. Underhill, an Anglican poet and journalist, wrote the classic *Mysticism* (1911), which is still in print and widely read by students of mysticism. It is a thorough and highly sympathetic handling of the subject. Underhill's older friend and adviser, Friedrich von Hügel, was a Catholic layman scholar who was favorably impressed by Hocking's work *The Meaning of God in*

[4] Margaret Lewis Furse, *Mysticism: Window on a World View* (Nashville: Abingdon Press, 1977), Chapter 5, "Premises of Modern Interpretation," pp. 129–49; Chapter 6, "Classic Modern Interpreters," pp. 150–72.

Human Experience.[5] Mainly von Hügel was critical of a mystical ontology that pressed so hard to unify all diversities that it ended in a world-denying zero. The mystic should seek the One, not as a geometrical conception, but as a unity that is analogous to the personality—a unity-in-diversity. (This conception is quite close to Hocking's "principle of alternation" described in Chapter 6.) William Ralph Inge, the Anglican dean of St. Paul's, was an eminent Platonist scholar and a prolific essayist and newspaper columnist. "Mysticism," he said, "has its origin in that which is the raw material of all religion, and perhaps of all philosophy and art as well, namely, that dim consciousness of the *beyond,* which is part of our nature as human beings. . . ."[6] The best sort of mysticism is Platonism, he thought, and accordingly there can be no conflict between mysticism and reason understood in a Platonist sense.

Among American interpreters, in addition to James and Hocking we need to mention the Quaker scholar Rufus Jones, the personalist James Bissett Pratt, and the psychologist James Leuba. Jones was a student of Josiah Royce and of George Herbert Palmer. He was himself something of a mystic. Among his historical works were *Studies in Mystical Religion* (1909) and *The Flowering of Mysticism: The Friends of God in the Fourteenth Century* (1939). James Bissett Pratt was a representative of the American school of personal idealism. The school as a whole was not typically sympathetic to the subject of mysticism since the mystics' "One" seemed to engulf the individuality of persons—a special emphasis of the school. Pratt, however, in *Religious Consciousness: A Psychological Study* (1920) tried to do what James had done: stop asking the presumably unanswerable question about the truth and verifiability of belief and simply take religious consciousness or experience as the subject of investigation. Not doctrine but *religiousness* was his subject. He also wrote *The Pilgrimage of Buddhism and a Buddhist Pilgrimage* (1928). James Leuba was one of the few who wrote about mysticism in a tone of hostility. His *Psychology of Religious Mysticism* (1926) focused on the psychological aberration of some of the mystics.

A number of factors influenced the way many of these early twentieth century studies were undertaken. As we have said, the need to accommodate religion and a modernist outlook was one factor that made mysticism an attractive subject. Writing in 1914, William Ralph Inge said that the study of a less doctrinal, more mystical type of religion brings a "relief to many who have been distressed by being told that religion is bound up with certain

---

[5] In 1923, when von Hügel wrote the Preface to the second edition of *The Mystical Element of Religion,* he had a word of appreciation for Hocking's work. Both Hocking and von Hügel would agree that to regard total disengagement from this world and its affairs was a mistake of nihilistic mysticism.

[6] William Ralph Inge, *Christian Mysticism* (London: Methuen & Co., 1948), p. 5.

events in antiquity, the historicity of which it is in some cases difficult to establish; with a cosmology which has been definitely disproved; and with a philosophy which they cannot make their own."[7] While Hocking rejected an outright identification of religion and feeling (if feeling is held to exclude idea), he said that locating religion in feeling does make us more comfortable about revelation because we are more diffident than our forefathers were about "lump-communications from behind the veil."[8]

One way to avoid a narrow dogmatism thus seemed to be a broadly empirical approach to religion. And when one considers religious *experience*, one is led directly to the classic reporters of religious experiences, the mystics. The comparatively new science of psychology, and James's application of it to religion, provided a new set of interpretive tools. And Henri Bergson, who influenced many in this group—especially James—provided a new approach to metaphysics. He described Being as a dynamic process discerned in its wholeness only by intuition. Logic and intellection dismember the whole and cut us off from access to it.

A common premise of these modern interpreters was that mystical experience could tell us something about a transcendent reality to which all human beings might have access, but from which conceptual language, with what von Hügel called its "hard rind," tended to cut us off. A recurring problem for all students of mysticism—realists, pragmatists, or idealists— was how to interpret the mystics' way of knowing inasmuch as it often entailed the negation of all predication applicable to God. Any interpretation of mysticism will have some theory of knowledge and of experience at the center of its interest.

In what lies just ahead we will find that James, as an empiricist, deals with mysticism primarily as a state of consciousness rather than as a doctrine or a metaphysical theory. His examination of it is of one piece with his evaluation of religious experience generally. Royce, the idealist, is not unappreciative of mysticism as experience, but he mainly examines mysticism as a theory of being and finds it to be a spiritual version of realism, which he finds self-contradictory. Hocking is an eclectic thinker. He is an Absolute idealist like Royce, but he adapts from James a pragmatic validation that he calls "negative pragmatism." By ît he means that whatever is irrelevant and utterly useless to life here and now cannot possibly be "true." Hocking will argue strongly, it so happens, for just that mystical realism that Royce rejects as self-contradictory.

James's analysis of mysticism is difficult and perhaps impossible to distinguish from his general treatment of religious experience. If it differs, it

---

[7] William Ralph Inge, "Institutionalism and Mysticism," in *Outspoken Essays*, Vol. 1, (New York: Longmans, Green and Co., 1927), pp. 230–31.

[8] William Ernest Hocking, *The Meaning of God in Human Experience* (New Haven: Yale University Press, 1912), p. 53.

differs only slightly. Mysticism, James holds, is that in which "personal religious experience has its root and centre."[9] James as an empiricist is open to consider any sort of religious experience, rational or irrational, that human beings report having. Does mystical experience tell us anything certain about reality itself? No, says James. The mystic's experience is authoritative only for the mystic; it gives us no access to universal or certain truth. Mystical experience, and religious experience generally, "may" give us access to a spiritual "more" of which we can be dimly aware as an extension of our conscious self beyond the margin of conceptual thinking. We are justi- fied, and James thinks better off, if we act on the hypothesis that this unseen world is real.

James is far less disturbed about mysticism's possible "irrationality" and negative predication than is an idealist like Royce. The reason is that James entertains no hope for metaphysical predication in the first place. For him experience is largely what reality is, and in *Varieties of Religious Experience*, religious experience is whatever religious individuals report it as being. Experience itself, as an undifferentiated dynamic manifold, as a "stream of consciousness," is as inaccessible to conceptual thought as is the mystics' idea of God. James is more responsible than anyone in this period for widening the notion of what experience is.

We will find in James's theory of knowing an interesting dualism. There is both a prospective outlook in James and also an immediatism. (In Chapter 6, we will see that Hocking falls heir to a similar sort of dualism.) By taking a prospective stance, James plays the role of the pragmatic empiricist and looks to experience to validate the hypothesis being tested. Sometimes James writes as if the experiential confirmation should come at a specifiable time and place.[10] At other times James seems to make the confirming empirical evidence lie in a general improvement in one's outlook and character. From a narrower empirical perspective that expects more precision, one would be justified in asking James when and where in the stream of life is there evidence specific enough to furnish real empirical confirmation. (Hocking is open to this same query.)

In the other feature of James's thought, called by Ralph Barton Perry "Immediatism," we find James impatient with conceptual knowledge be-

---

[9] William James, *The Varieties of Religious Experience* (New York: Collier, 1961), p. 299.
[10]   There can *be* no difference anywhere that doesn't *make* a difference elsewhere—no difference in abstract truth that doesn't express itself in a difference in concrete fact and in conduct consequent upon that fact, imposed on somebody, somehow, somewhere, and somewhen. The whole function of philosophy ought to be to find out what definite difference it will make to you and me, at definite instants of our life, if this world-formula or that world formula be the true one.

    —William James, "What Pragmatism Means," in John K. Roth (ed.), *The Moral Philosophy of William James* (New York: Thomas Y. Crowell, 1969), p. 278.

cause it chops into pieces the whole mainfold or stream of experience. There is a "direct acquaintance" that he regards as superior to merely indirect, conceptual ways of knowing.

These tendencies, both of which are visible in *Varieties of Religious Experience*, can lead to an anti-intellectualism in James that is very much lamented by Royce and Hocking. We will consider these issues again after we have reviewed the lectures that James's Edinburgh audience listened to with great interest in 1901.

Varieties of Religious Experience

James's Gifford Lectures, *Varieties of Religious Experience*, begin with a denunciation of what he calls "medical materialism." By that phrase James meant a dogmatism of a materialistic rather than an ecclesiastical kind. James abhorred every sort of dogmatism and thought that all of them tended to explain an idea's worth by looking back to that idea's origin or cause. Ecclesiastical dogmatism would interpret an idea's worth in terms of some institutional or revelatory origin. The dogmatism of medical materialism would discredit a religious experience by attributing its origin to some prior pathological condition of the brain.

James holds that the antidote to this sort of dogmatism is the prospective stance of empiricism: Look to the effects and not to the source to make your evaluation. "By their fruits ye shall know them, not by their roots."[11] Just what constitutes these authenticating fruits or empirical results and whether they are so clearly specifiable in a whole life's experience that they can serve as empirical validation are questions to consider. But as James begins *Varieties*, he greatly stresses a prospective validating test, and he rejects any validation drawn from authority of the past.

One of James's most frequently quoted working definitions of religion is: "The feelings, acts and experiences of individual men in their solitude, so far as they apprehend themselves to stand in whatever they consider divine."[12] From it we can see how intent he is to avoid discussing the authority of stated theological beliefs as developed in religious institutions. Here he tries to keep to what would now be called a phenomenological approach by bracketing the question of whether the individuals are right in "whatever they consider divine."[13] While eventually in *Varieties*, James does speculate about the truth-claim implied by religious experience, in this definition and almost throughout these lectures, he offers descriptions of individual religious experience as it is reported by those individuals.

---

[11] James, *Varieties*, p. 34.

[12] Ibid., p. 42.

[13] See Bruce Wilshire, *William James and Phenomenology: A Study of "The Principles of Psychology"* (Bloomington: Indiana University Press, 1968).

Another feature of the definition is that James appears to think that he must, in order to be empirical, stick to the *individual's* religious experience and avoid, as much as possible, institutional forms of religion. One of the often observed limitations of *Varieties* is its almost exclusive interest in the experiential reports of individuals and the neglect of the group. The empirical study of religious institutions, as in sociology of religion, for example, was simply not an avenue of inquiry for James.

Another definition that James suggests is that religion might possibly be "man's total reaction upon life"—but a total reaction with a certain reverential quality. Regardless of whether the total reaction is theistic, James still holds it to be religious unless it lacks the reverential attitude necessary to religion. Such an attitude cannot be a shrugging "Who cares?" in the manner of Voltaire. It must, if it is a religious attitude, be "solemn, serious, and tender." "If glad, it must not grin or snicker; if sad it must not scream or curse." What the "divine" should be held to mean, then, is "such a primal reality as the individual feels impelled to respond to solemnly and gravely, and neither by a curse nor a jest."[14]

This religious attitude James distinguishes from a moral or moralistic attitude. Morality and religion are related, but they are not identical. Religion means an "enthusiastic temper of espousal" rather than a stoicism with "muscles tense." We can see this, says James—and he spoke from personal experience—when we have become morally exhausted in our attempt to renew moral effort. Then "our morality appears as a plaster hiding a sore it can never cure." But there is a state of mind known to religious persons, and not to moralists, in which moral assertion "has been displaced by a willingness to . . . be as nothing in the floods and waterspouts of God." It is a time for tension to be over, a time "of happy relaxation, of calm deep breathing, of an eternal present, with no discordant future to be anxious about."[15]

We have to note in passing that as James here distinguishes religion from morality, he also tends to describe religion in terms of a quietism of the sort celebrated by mystics. James has also moved here from the prospective stance that expects specific validation in terms of "a difference in concrete fact and in conduct consequent upon that fact."[16] Now he celebrates immediacy in which consolation is presently experienced. In fairness we must add, however, that here he is describing the religious attitude, and not offering it as a validating effect.

Still another definition of "the life of religion" is that "it consists of the belief that there is an unseen order, and that our supreme good lies in harmoniously adjusting ourselves thereto." In the many interesting personal

---

[14]James, *Varieties*, pp. 46, 47, 48.
[15]Ibid., pp. 55, 54.
[16]William James, "Pragmatism," in John K. Roth (ed.), *The Moral Philosophy of William James* (New York: Thomas Y. Crowell, 1969), p. 278.

histories that James reports (most of which we omit in this review), he draws
the conclusion that whether the individuals are right or wrong in reporting
their sense of "the reality of the unseen," they are always absolutely convinced personally of its reality. They are not, however, according to James,
convinced by argument or analysis. "Instinct leads, intelligence does but
follow. If a person feels the presence of a living God . . . your critical
arguments . . . will vainly set themselves to change his faith." He adds that it
may not be "better that the subconscious and non-rational should thus hold
primacy in the religious realm." He means simply to point out "that they do
so hold as a matter of fact."[17]

One of the especially interesting features of *Varieties of Religious Experience* is James's analysis of that religious change in a person's life called
"conversion." He analyzes this change through certain psychological principles, some of which he himself had developed (and in 1890 had described in
his *Principles of Psychology*) and some of which—theories of the unconscious—were then relatively new. As a preparation for the discussion of
conversion, it is necessary to have in view the two religious personality types
or "temperaments" James identified, the second of which is especially open
to conversion.

The "once-born" personality type is the person whose temperament of
"healthy mindedness" tends toward a spiritual contentment and a disinclina-
tion toward change or religious conversion. There is a natural happiness
already in place. There is no overwhelming sense of suffering or morbidity of
mind that demands escape or rescue. As examples James cites Walt Whit-
man, and he quotes the astonishingly untroubled Unitarian minister, Ed-
ward Everett Hale:

> I always knew God loved me, and I was always grateful to him
> for the world he placed me in. . . . I had no idea whatever
> what the problem of life was. To live with all my might seemed
> to me easy; to learn where there was so much to learn seemed
> pleasant and almost of course; to lend a hand, if one had a
> chance, natural; and if one did this, why, he enjoyed life
> because he could not help it, and without proving to himself
> that he ought to enjoy it. . . .[18]

But James did not find this "sky-blue" temperament nearly as "complete" as the second type, that of the "sick soul" or the "morbid minded"
person who feels the need of being "twice-born." To the twice-born temperament evil is a vividly discomforting reality and there can be a desperate need
to escape from it. Tolstoy's condition is an example of such a state. "I felt,"

[17]James, *Varieties*, pp. 59, 75.
[18]Ibid., p. 81.

said Tolstoy, "that something had broken within me on which my life had always rested, that I had nothing left to hold on to, and that morally my life had stopped."[19]

Conversion is the religious name for the twice-born soul's experience of deliverance from such a morbid-minded state. The change represented in conversion, as it is described by individuals reporting their religious experiences, is much more radical and complex, says James, than simply a return to good health and outlook. "The process is one of redemption, not of mere reversion to natural health, and the sufferer, when saved, is saved by what seems to him a second birth, a deeper kind of conscious being than he could enjoy before."[20] Here is the way Tolstoy describes his own recovery:

> I was alone in the forest, lending my ear to its mysterious noises. I listened, and my thought went back to what for these three years it always was busy with—the quest of God. But the idea of him, I said, how did I ever come by the idea?
>
> And again there arose in me, with this thought, glad aspirations towards life. Everything in me awoke and received a meaning. . . . Why do I look farther? a voice within me asked. He is there: he, without whom one cannot live. To acknowledge God and to live are one and the same. . . .
>
> After this, things cleared up within me and about me better than ever, and the light has never wholly died away.[21]

In discussing conversion James, so far at least, intends to be descriptive and to offer suggestions from psychology to help explain the mechanism of the change of focus called conversion. He does not use the conversion experience as any sort of argument for the existence of God. As explanatory tools he uses his own theory of "stream of consciousness" and "field of consciousness" developed in the *Principles of Psychology* and the theories of "subliminal" or subconscious mind. Among the new theorists of the unconscious whom he credits are Binet, Janet, Breuer, Freud, Mason, Prince, and Myers. James's acceptance of the theory of the unconscious was new for him. At the time of his *Principles of Psychology*, he had rejected the notion because it would make of psychology, instead of a science, a "tumbling ground for whimsies" where anything could be true.[22]

In his *Principles of Psychology*, James had described conscious life, in his famous metaphor, as a "stream" or "river" of consciousness. We experience

[19] Ibid., p. 133. James describes his own experience of morbid-mindedness as that of a "Frenchman," p. 138.

[20] Ibid., p. 135.

[21] Ibid., p. 157.

[22] Ibid., p. 193; Marcus Peter Ford, *William James's Philosophy: A New Perspective* (Amherst: University of Massachusetts Press, 1982), p. 19.

not just those static entities for which we have names—the "resting places," or the "substantive parts." We also experience the "transitions" or relations between the substantive parts. We do not experience reality atomized. We have it presented to us, before our selecting process begins, in a whole moving wave or stream. But when the self selects, names a thing, identifies a substance, or says "here" or "this" or "mine," what is taking place, according to James, is a focusing of the attention on certain segments of the stream which are central to our present interest. And we relegate to a "corner of the eye" other segments of the stream.

It is possible, of course, to change our interest and our focus or "field of consciousness." Objects once peripheral may become central and vice versa. For example, James recalls for his audience how the subject of the Gifford Lectures had moved, in his own consciousness, from the margin to the center. "I remember my father reading aloud from a Boston newspaper that part of Lord Gifford's will which founded these four lectureships. . . . What I listened to [then] was as remote . . . as if it related to Mars. Yet here I am, with the Gifford system part and parcel of my very self."[23]

So the process of experiencing is a process of selecting and refocusing one's attention. This refocusing is brought about by "the way in which irrational excitement alters. Things hot and vital to us today are cold tomorrow." The hot part of a person's field of consciousness is "the habitual centre of his personal energy."[24] It is that part of experience in which a person has a stake or an "interest."

What happens in a person's religious conversion, then, is "that religious ideas previously peripheral in . . . consciousness, now take central place and . . . form the habitual centre of his energy." Although psychology can describe the mechanism of change, it cannot really say why the change takes place. It is as if a new meaning for an old thought "peals through us for the first time." Habits and formal associations of ideas retard the change. Such things as new information, violent emotions, and the brooding anxiety of adolescence, accelerate it. The change often seems both to the person undergoing it and also to onlookers to have some mysterious "element of marvel."[25]

In his *Principles of Psychology,* James had thought, as we have mentioned, that the empiricism he espoused would necessarily rule out the existence of an unconscious mind. In *Varieties,* however, he uses the hot center–cold periphery metaphor so as to blur and even efface the boundary line of consciousness. There is, as he now holds in *Varieties,* an "unconscious cerebration" which is "extra-marginal."[26] The field of consciousness and of

[23] James, *Varieties,* p. 164.
[24] Ibid., pp. 164, 165.
[25] Ibid., pp. 165, 166, 167.
[26] Ibid., pp. 173, 191.

possible experience is now vastly enlarged by the addition of the unconscious. It is also necessarily made more mysterious, which is to say less
accessible to conceptual thought. In *A Pluralistic Universe* James writes:

> My present field of consciousness is a centre surrounded by a
> fringe that shades insensibly into the subconscious more. I use
> three separate terms here to describe this fact; but I might as
> well use three hundred, for the fact is all shades and no
> boundaries. Which part of it properly is in my consciousness,
> which out? If I name what is out, it already has come in. The
> centre works in one way while the margins work in another,
> and presently overpower the centre and are central them-
> selves. What we conceptually identify ourselves with and say
> we are thinking of . . . is the centre, but our *full* self is the
> whole field with . . . subconscious possibilities . . . that we
> can hardly begin to analyze.[27]

Here James has set things up for what is usually called the "anti-
intellectualist" or nonconceptual turn in his thought. And he has radically
enlarged the self and the self's experience. The conscious life, moreover, is
seen to be open to "incursions" from the unconscious that can motivate or
inhibit actions and even produce hallucination or obsessive ideas and be-
havior. If, then, the mechanism of conversion is not dissimilar from certain
pathological changes caused by these unconscious incursions, how is religious conversion to be evaluated? Are there genuine and are there counterfeit conversions?

In the evangelical church circles of James's day, it was the suddenness of
the conversion that gave it more claim to validity. James discounts this sort of
criterion and returns to his prospective stance, that of judging by the "fruits"
and not by the "roots." "If the *fruits for life* of the state of conversion are
good, we ought to idealize and venerate it, even though it be a piece of
natural psychology; if not, we ought to make short work with it, no matter
what supernatural being may have infused it."[28]

"Conversion," then, is the religious name for the sick soul's recovery, the
"twice-born's" second birth. And it occurs by a refocusing of the field of
consciousness and by the incursion into it of impulses from a subliminal
region beyond the "margin" of consciousness. James concludes his discussion
of conversion with a hypothesis: "*If there be* higher spiritual agencies that
can directly touch us, the psychological condition of their doing so *might be*
our possession of a subconscious region which alone should yield access to
them."[29] The proper "test of religion," however, has nothing to do with how

[27] Bruce Wilshire (ed.), *William James: The Essential Writings* (Albany: State University of
New York Press, 1984), p. 365.
[28] James, *Varieties*, p. 195.
[29] Ibid., p. 198.

these psychological changes occur, but with "something ethical definable only in terms of *what is attained*."[30]

What, then, in an ethical sense is attained by religious conversion?

These "fruits" or effects of conversion James calls "saintliness" or "sanctification." "Saintliness" is "the collective name for the ripe fruits of religion in a character." James describes these as (a) a feeling of living in a wider world than one's own selfish interests; (b) a sense of "friendly continuity" and therefore willing self-surrender to an ideal power; (c) elation, freedom; and (d) a shift of the emotional center toward loving and harmonious affections. These are the empirical fruits of religion evident in a person's character.

These religious effects are, however, not always an unmixed good. In some personalities one or another of the virtues of saintliness may be so exaggerated that the personality becomes unbalanced and excessively zealous. For example, the virtue of self-surrender may be pushed to the point of fanatical asceticism. The sense of elation and freedom may completely annul the sense of responsibility for this world because the world, by comparison with the elation, seems too insignificant.

The qualities of character that are here described are psychological effects and do not, in themselves, entitle us to say whether "God exists." James holds that religions and gods are in fact historically and actually judged in terms of human values. Historically those deities and religions that thwart or conflict with "indispensible human ideals" become discredited, neglected, and forgotten. "When we cease to admire or approve what the definition of a deity implies, we end by deeming that deity incredible." This way of judging is no more than "the survival of the humanly fittest, applied to religious beliefs." This way of judging gives only a rough guide, he admits. But it is the sort of guide we use in every day life where we make "piecemeal judgments" in which "our general philosophical prejudices, our instincts, and our common sense are our only guides." In this rough way we are to "decide that *on the whole* one type of religion is approved by its fruits, and another type condemned."[31]

As James leaves the subject of saintliness, which raised the question of the moral "utility" of religion, he now turns to the subject of mysticism itself and to the question of whether any possible "truth" might be found in religious experience. Or rather, we should say, he explores those religious experiences called "mysticism" in which some persons have "professed to see truth in a special manner."[32]

James thinks of mysticism as that in which "personal religious experience has its root and centre."[33] In James's well-known definition of what he will

---

[30] Ibid., p. 197. James here quotes George E. Coe, *The Spiritual Life* (New York), 1900.
[31] James, *Varieties*, pp. 262, 263, 265, 261–262.
[32] Ibid., p. 298.
[33] Ibid., p. 299.

mean by the mystical state of consciousness, he proposes four "marks": ineffability, noetic quality, transiency, and passivity. In specifying these it is clear that he has in mind an empirically describable state of consciousness and not a metaphysical system or world view.

James gives as the simplest example of mystical experience the common one in which a word or a phrase suddenly has a new significance. The dejá vù feeling is another example; still another is the sense, when enjoying a natural setting, that "everything I see has a meaning, if I could but understand it."[34]

In looking to the effect rather than to the origin for the validation of an idea, James was free to name "mystical" any state that achieved the marks of mysticism regardless of its cause. "The drunken consciousness is one bit of the mystical consciousness," he said. "Nitrous oxide and ether, especially nitrous oxide, when diluted with air, stimulate the mystical consciousness in an extraordinary degree." Drug-induced states were not a central feature of James's study of mysticism, but his prospective, pragmatic stance did allow their inclusion. He himself experimented with nitrous oxide and offered this description: "One conclusion was forced upon my mind at the time, and my impression of its truth has ever since remained unshaken. It is that our normal waking consciousness, rational consciousness as we call it, is but one special type of consciousness, whilst all about it, parted from it by the filmiest of screens, there lie potential forms of consciousness entirely different."[35]

The various religions—Hinduism, Buddhism, and Christianity—are found to have a method of instruction for the "methodical cultivation" of mystical states. But James thinks that these various methods all end in the same result, an incommunicable transport, which he finds the "keynote" of all mysticism. "I had learned that words could teach of Sufism," said Al Ghazzali, "but what was left could be learned neither by study nor through the ears, but solely by giving one's self up to ecstasy and leading a pious life."[36]

Are such ineffable mystical states, then, in any sense "authoritative" in warranting truth? James gives his answer in three succinct points:

---

[34] Ibid., p. 303.

[35] Ibid., p. 305. For an indication of James's interest in exceptional mental states and psychical research see Gardner Murphy and Robert Ballou (eds.), *William James on Psychical Research* (New York: Viking Press, 1960), and Eugene Taylor, *William James on Exceptional Mental States: The 1896 Lowell Lectures* (Amherst: University of Massachusetts Press, 1984). One of James's reasons for giving readers of *Varieties of Religious Experience* his "four marks" of mystical experience was to dissociate the word "mystic" from faddist interpretations of it. He writes, "For some writers a 'mystic' is any person who believes in thought-transference, or spirit-return. Employed in this way the word has little value: there are many less ambiguous synonyms." *Varieties*, p. 299.

[36] Ibid., p. 317.

1. Mystical states are "and have the right to be" authoritative for the individual who has them. Our own more "rational beliefs," James says, are "based on evidence exactly similar," which is to say on "direct perceptions of fact."

2. They are not binding on those who "stand outside of them."

3. "They break down the authority of the non-mystical or rationalistic consciousness, based upon the understanding and the senses alone. They show it to be only one kind of consciousness. They open out the possibility of other orders of truth, in which so far as anything in us vitally responds to them, we may freely continue to have faith."[37]

James leaves us only with a possibility but with no certainties. It is possible that mystical states are like windows to a more extensive and inclusive world which the rationalistic critic cannot really deny a priori. He concludes that "it may be that possibility and permission of this sort are all that our religious consciousness requires to live on."[38]

In *Varieties of Religious Experience*, the recurring question, many times deferred in favor of experiential description, is "Is the sense of divine presence a sense of anything objectively true?" Mysticism is found to be too private to claim universal authority. What about philosophy? Will it give a warrant to the truth of the religious person's sense of the divine? As James raises this question, he makes an admission to his audience: "You suspect that I am planning to defend feeling at the expense of reason, to rehabilitate the primitive and unreflective, and to dissuade you from the hope of any Theology. . . . I have to admit that you guess rightly. I do believe that feeling is the deeper source of religion, and that philosophic and theologic formulas are secondary products like translations of a text into another tongue."[39]

Without religious feeling James thinks that it is doubtful that any philosophical theology could have been developed. "I doubt if dispassionate intellectual contemplation of the universe apart from inner unhappiness and need for deliverance on the one hand and mystical emotion on the other, would ever have resulted in religious philosophies such as we now possess." The kind of intellectualism that James wants to discredit here is that represented by scholasticism and Absolute idealism. Both pit "feeling valid for the individual" against "reason valid universally." But, says James, the arguments for the existence of God do not convince "unless you have a God already whom you believe in."[40] He regards the arguments of Absolute idealism (and he uses the example of Principal John Caird rather than Royce) as simply a reaffirming of the individual's experiences in a more generalized

[37] Ibid., pp. 331, 332.
[38] Ibid., p. 336.
[39] Ibid., p. 337.
[40] Ibid., pp. 338, 341, 342.

vocabulary. Argument does not establish the truth of religion by coercive reasoning.[41]

What religion reports is a fact of experience: that the divine is actually present. If knowledge of this divine is possible, it must be a matter of "definite perceptions of fact." Conceptual knowledge can only class facts and interpret them, but it cannot produce them. "There is always a *plus*, a *thisness*, which feeling alone can answer for. Philosophy in this sphere is a secondary function, unable to warrant faith's veracity. . . ." Philosophy ought to abandon metaphysics in favor of criticism and induction "and frankly transform herself from theology into science of religions." James concludes: "In all sad sincerity I think we must conclude that the attempt to demonstrate by purely intellectual processes the truth of the deliverances of direct religious experience is absolutely hopeless."[42]

Is there any sort of common religious belief? James's answer is yes, but his description of it is pared down to paper-thin proportions. The common religious creed consists of two parts: (a) an uneasiness, and (b) its solution. In the solution there is the sense of being saved from some wrongness by making a connection with higher powers. Religious persons become conscious that this higher part of themselves "*is coterminous and continuous with a* MORE *of the same quality which is operative in the universe. . . .*"[43]

Is this "more" merely our own notion or does it really exist? James answers here by suggesting that this "more" is the unconscious self, the existence of which shows that there is actually and literally more life in the total self than we can be aware of. James cannot really say what this "more" is "on its farther side." But "on its hither side" it is, he thinks, the "subconscious continuation of our conscious life."[44] He thinks the religious person's sense of union with a power beyond is, therefore, a solid reality, provided we hold that power to be the unconscious continuation of the self.

It is not possible to achieve any universally true statement about the "more" on the farther side. We have to be content with allowing a pluralism of individual beliefs about it. That the individual is justified in entertaining such beliefs is a point on which James is very clear. These beliefs, adopted by freely choosing to go beyond the minimal creed (above), James calls "over-beliefs." They are, he thinks, "absolutely indispensable."[45]

In offering his own personal "over-beliefs," James enlists himself with "the supernaturalists" in that he himself believes in the reality of the un-

[41] Ibid., p. 354.
[42] Ibid., pp. 354, 355.
[43] Ibid., pp. 393–394. James's emphasis.
[44] Ibid., p. 396.
[45] Ibid., p. 398.

seen—a "mystical region" or a "supernatural region."[46] He even enlists with what he calls supernaturalists of the "crasser" kind—those who expect the unseen world to produce real effects in this one. It is clear, though, that the kind of real effects he has in mind are changes in character and moral outlook.

James himself says that he prefers to call the higher reality "God" rather than "Over-Soul" because he thinks the transcendentalists usually mean by Over-Soul only an ineffective medium of communion without causal agency. We are not to suppose, necessarily, that the higher power is infinite or monistic. It may even be only a higher, more godlike self, and the universe may be a collection of such selves. The most that can be claimed as a conclusion is this hypothesis: "Something ideal, which in one sense is part of ourselves and in another sense is not ourselves, actually exerts an influence, raises our center of personal energy, and produces regenerative effects unattainable in other ways. . . . At these places at least, I say, it would seem as though transmundane energies, God, if you will, produced immediate effects within the natural world to which the rest of our experience belongs."[47]

The Outcome

Finally, then, when we have finished *Varieties of Religious Experience* and asked James where we stand, it is certainly not possible to find his answer given with a slogan. He holds that rationalists are not justified in overturning religious belief on their grounds alone. On the other hand, reason cannot prove the religious hypothesis either. Since he supposedly knows from psychological research that there are subliminal, extramarginal spheres of consciousness, who is to say that a larger spiritual world with regenerative energy might not lie beyond that subliminal margin? It is certainly possible, says James, that the farther side of consciousness may be the source of those more generous feelings and healthier outlooks he has described in his numerous case studies. At least, we are justified, he tells us, in hypothesizing that there is an unseen world and that a real difference is actually made in our lives here and now because of the way we adjust ourselves to that unseen world. But James holds us strictly to the subjunctive mood of possibility and offers no certainty. He asks us to look for the empirical effects of the religious hypothesis in the sphere of moral life and character. And in such a sphere the evidence is never complete.

---

[46] Ibid., p. 399. Of the effects of the unseen world, James says, "When we commune with it, work is actually done upon our finite personality, for we are turned into new men and consequences in the way of conduct follow in the natural world upon our regenerative change." James, *Varieties*, p. 399. Compare John Dewey, *A Common Faith*.

[47] James, *Varieties*, p. 405.

James's many suggestions do not all lead in the same direction; yet it would be small-minded to say of his experimental philosophical style that there are "major inconsistencies." We can point to two directions in his thought which are apparent in *Varieties of Religious Experience* and which are also represented in various of his other works. We will also find a version of these two tendencies in Hocking's empirical idealism; so it will be worthwhile to illustrate them here in James.

In the first tendency, the prospective outlook, the key ideal is the empirical justification of belief in its fruits or results. The other tendency, immediatism, focuses on experience as a whole and concludes that it can be accessed only by direct acquaintance and not by intellection. Belief, prospect, and risk-taking in behalf of an idea are the key elements of the prospective outlook. Religious experience (rather than belief), immediacy, consolation, and the inadequacy of conceptual knowledge are the key elements in immediatism.

Both of these tendencies can eventuate in an anti-intellectualism for somewhat different reasons. The prospective tendency can land there because in the sphere of religion and moral life the looked-for evidence can never be complete. It becomes necessary then to act in the absence of evidence and take a risk for the religious hypothesis. This is the program of James's essay "The Will to Believe." Immediatism tends toward anti-intellectualism because the reality, the stream of consciousness, is too dynamic for conceptual knowledge.

The prospective outlook is illustrated by the reason that James gives in *Varieties of Religious Experience* for judging that medical materialism is wrong. Medical materialism looks backward rather than forward. In looking ahead, what ought one to look for? Look for a shift in one's affections to more generous and psychologically comfortable ones. This shift does not constitute a proof for the existence of God, but proofs only appeal anyway, says James, to persons whose feelings already dispose them to act in behalf of their religious idea. Thus belief is a matter of living life forward and taking a risk in behalf of a religious idea despite the absence of proof. As a definition of faith James gives us the following: "Faith means belief in something concerning which doubt is still theoretically possible; and as the test of the belief is willingness to act, one may say that faith is the readiness to act in a cause the prosperous issue of which is not certified in advance."[48] As there is no proof and no certainty, a risk attends belief. In James's famous essay, "The Will to Believe," he certainly makes it clear that the risk in behalf of belief is worth the taking. (See note for the gist of the essay.)[49]

---

[48] William James, "The Sentiment of Rationality," in *The Will to Believe and Other Essays in Popular Philosophy* (New York: Dover Publications, Inc., 1956), p. 90.

[49] References within this note are to James's essay, "The Will to Believe" in Roth (ed.), *The Moral Philosophy of William James* (New York: Thomas Y. Crowell, 1969). In it, he holds that in

This prospective tendency that represents a theme in James's thought is also illustrated in his theory of truth and of the relation of ideas to objects. We shall mention the theory briefly because Royce sees the linkage between an idea and its object in a similarly prospective way.

What makes an idea "true" of its object? The answer that James gives is that the idea comes into being in the first place because the person who entertains it has a purpose or practical motive in mind. The intention of the knower provides the linkage between idea and object. The idea is like a tool in aid of getting to an intended terminus. Suppose I have an idea of "tigers in India." I intend for the idea to be useful for my purpose in coming face-to-face with tigers when I go to the actual India.[50] Why is it that I know that the real tigers in the real India are the proper terminus of my idea? What, in other words, makes the idea "true" of its object? The reason lies in my original intention, and I know what that is. I have selected the idea to stand for this face-to-face confrontation with tigers; I am, therefore, able to recognize the fulfillment of my idea's purpose when it does come in experience.

---

the case of religion the validating evidence is never complete. Nevertheless we are, under circumstances of "momentous" importance, justified in acting in advance of that evidence. For one thing, to withhold one's decision and to stand aloof is itself a decision. Decisions are, therefore, unavoidable, and in making them, we have two obligations: to know the truth and to avoid error. But in fulfilling both these obligations James says that we should not be so transfixed by the avoidance of error that we cut ourselves off from possible truths. The truth is never fixed and final "as if it never could be reinterpreted" (p. 201). The strict employment of the principle of parsimony only represents to James an inordinate fear of committing an error. W. K. Clifford, the writer whom James intended to refute in "Will to Believe," is quoted as saying that "it is wrong always, everywhere, and for everyone, to believe anything upon insufficient evidence" (p. 197). To this James replies that we have no certainties anyway, and so "our errors are surely not such awfully solemn things. In a world where we are so certain to incur them in spite of all our caution, a certain lightness of heart seems healthier than this excessive nervousness on their behalf" (p. 204).

James thinks that in the moral and religious sphere we are better off adopting the belief-option because acting in that idea's behalf is the only way to test the idea. Moreover, acting as if the idea were true may effectively bring into being that which is believed: My believing that you like me effectively makes you like me. If I stand aloof to have your liking proved, chances are it will never come. My believing in a personal God may open to me the benefits (of saintliness of character, generous affections, solace) that would come in case there is such a God. If we fail to risk acting in behalf of belief then we shut ourselves up in "snarling logicality" and try to make God "extort" our recognition. Then we have cut ourselves off from all "opportunities of making the god's acquaintance," if there should be a God (p. 211). James does not reckon with the possible claim of atheism to be a positive belief in behalf of which one might venture to act and conceivably derive benefits thereby. For a criticism of the argument see Morton White, *Science and Sentiment in America* (New York: Oxford University Press, 1972), pp. 188–201. See also the especially thorough treatment, James C. S. Wernham, *James's Will-to-Believe Doctrine: A Heretical View* (Kingston-Montreal: McGill-Queen's University Press, 1987).

[50] Ralph Barton Perry, *Present Philosophical Tendencies* (New York: Longmans, Green and Co., 1929), p. 358.

We should note, in passing, that James keeps the intentionality and its fulfillment within the finite individual's experience or "possible" experience. Royce, as we will see, will require the experience of the Absolute in order to secure idea-object linkage. Hocking will assert that knowledge of objects and of other selves is based on our immediate and certain apprehension of God.

The second tendency in James, that of immediatism, is the outlook that prefers direct acquaintance rather than "knowledge about." In *The Principles of Psychology*, James had identified consciousness as a dynamic process of experience: "Consciousness does not appear to itself chopped up in bits. Such words as 'chain' or 'train' do not describe it fitly as it presents itself in the first instance. It is nothing jointed; it flows. A 'river' or a 'stream' are the metaphors by which it is most naturally described. *In talking of it hereafter, let us call it the stream of thought, of consciousness, or of subjective life.*"[51] Once James describes experience as an unanalyzable dynamic manifold, then it seems to him that there must be a better route to it than through the intellect which dismembers it. Is there not a more direct, unmediated way? According to Ralph Barton Perry, James is the "only" pragmatist who makes nonintellectual experience a kind of knowledge. Knowledge mediated by ideas is for James only one way of knowing and not the most profound way. The best ideas for James would (quoting James) "lead to an actual merging of ourselves with the object, to an utter mutual confluence of identification."[52]

It is interesting to see how vigorous and active the self is held to be when the prospective outlook is in play. Then the volitional aspects of the self are emphasized. It selects out of experience what its own interest directs it to focus on. When, however, the immediatism of James is in effect, the self all but becomes absorbed into the undifferentiated stuff of experience and seems to drop out of sight. In *A Pluralistic Universe* we find James saying that "what we conceptually identify ourselves with and say we are thinking of at anytime is the centre [of consciousness]; but our *full* self is the whole field with all those indefinitely radiating subconscious possibilities of increase that we can only feel without conceiving, and can hardly begin to analyze."[53]

By either route, that of the prospective outlook or that of immediatism, we find James amazingly nonchalant in risking anti-intellectualism and

[51] Wilshire (ed.), *William James*, p. 53. James's emphasis.

[52] Perry, *Present Philosophical Tendencies*, p. 224; ibid., p. 156.

[53] Wilshire (ed.), *William James*, p. 365. In James's essay "Does Consciousness Exist?" from his *Essays in Radical Empiricism* we read:

> My thesis is that if we start with the supposition that there is only one primal stuff or material in the world, a stuff of which everything is composed, and if we call that stuff "pure experience," then knowing can easily be explained as a particular sort of relation towards one another into which portions of pure experience may enter. The relation itself is a part of pure experience; one of its "terms" becomes the subject or bearer of the knowledge, the knower, the other becomes the object known. (Ibid., p. 163).

positively accepting of the essential mystery at the core of the mystics' conception of reality. He says that "philosophy lives in words, but truth and fact well up into our lives in ways that exceed verbal formulation. There is in the act of perception always something that glimmers and twinkles and will not be caught, and for which reflection comes too late."[54] But as we shall see, James's friend Royce will never agree to any truth that only wells up into our lives or any truth so modest in its ambition that it proclaims itself to be a mere hypothesis. And Hocking will share Royce's dissatisfaction.

[54] James, *Varieties*, p. 356.

CHAPTER 3
ROYCE ON MYSTICISM

If the attentiveness of their respective audiences is any test, Royce's metaphysics must be a more tedious undertaking than James's method of psychological reporting. Having preceded James in the Gifford Lectures, Royce had thoughtfully told him what he might expect and warned him not to be disappointed if his audience began to lose interest and dwindled to about fifteen. But when James's turn came, he found himself with an audience of about 300 who listened attentively to his intriguing case studies.[1]

Royce began his lectures, *The World and the Individual,* in the customary fashion of his day, by rejecting several philosophical persuasions and then arguing for his own. He criticized three conceptions of being—realism, mysticism, and critical rationalism, and then he offered his own type of Absolute idealism as the "Fourth Conception of Being."

Mysticism is not the central feature of Royce's form of idealism as it is of Hocking's. Mysticism figures in Royce as one of the three theories of being he examines and criticizes. By and large, he interprets it as a type of metaphysics and epistemology. He finds it instructive both in the insights it positively offers and in its mistaken claims. Royce's sensitivity in interpreting mysticism is especially evident in the essay "Meister Eckhart," which we will look at later.

Royce did not share James's skepticism about conceptual thinking or James's belief that feeling rather than thought is the determiner of religious belief. Royce thought that truth needs to be systematically built up by a painstaking process of rational thought. Logical entailment is the mark of a valid method, and he disapproved of any method that short-circuited the serious intellectual work of discursive reasoning. He took the metaphysician's task seriously. Relying on a simply immediate experience was to shirk responsibility in favor of something unreliable. Royce said that immediate, intuitive forms of knowing, whether they are a realism or a mysticism, fail to notice that what is being compared is one idea with another and not, as is supposed, an idea and an object out there (realism) or "in thy heart" (mysticism). Mainly, then, Royce's quarrel with mysticism is that at bottom it is a form of realism or intuitive empiricism.

---

[1] Gay Wilson Allen, *William James: A Biography* (New York: Viking Press, 1967), p. 423.

We should now take a brief look at the four conceptions of being that Royce describes in *The World and the Individual*. Having a glimpse of his metaphysical aim, we can then return for a second, closer look at his analysis of mysticism. Of Royce's social philosophy, his concept of loyalty and of community, and his justification of evil, we cannot attempt to give an account here.

Royce's Four Conceptions of Being

Realism, the first theory of being that Royce examines, is the one farthest removed from his own. In much of what he writes, he seems preoccupied with this type of metaphysic and theory of knowing. It is always his real opponent, and in arguing for his own idealism, he frequently rehearses its weaknesses. One sometimes gets the impression that showing the weaknesses in realism is in itself enough to affirm the idealist position. In fact, he criticizes both mysticism and critical rationalism by regarding them as a variation of realism.

As Royce describes realism, it holds that the real is wholly independent of any ideas we have about it. "The real," says the realist philosopher, "is in one sense given, or immediate, just because no knowing process in us who know the object, creates, affects, or otherwise mediates the known real object. There it is, the real." For the realist the real is simply what is there whether or not we, as knowing beings, choose to pay attention to it or think about it or define it. To the realist the relation between the knower and the object known moves only in one direction: from object to knower. The relation of knower to real object Royce compares to that between "a horse and a hitching post."[2] The realist assumes that our act of knowing has absolutely no effect on the object known.

Royce finds that the trouble with realism is that it puts the aspiring knower in the position of trying to come into a relation with a real object which, by definition, is unrelated to the knowing process or to the knowing self. The relation between the object and the knower can never be accounted for on realistic premises. Nor can relations between object and object be accounted for. No causal relation can logically be imputed to objects. No variation or common characteristics may be asserted of them. And, therefore, no unity or continuity, and hence no order or meaning, can be asserted of the world of objects. Royce thinks that the "real" world, on the realist's premises, turns into "a chaos of unintelligible fragments and of scattered events," in which the knower faces what amounts to an unknown. "The realm of consistent Realism," he says, "is the realm of absolutely Nothing."[3]

---

[2] Josiah Royce, *The World and the Individual*, Vol. 1 (New York: The Macmillan Co., 1923), pp. 67, 70.

[3] Ibid., pp. 17, 137.

Mysticism, the second theory Royce examines, begins not like realism with an external object but with an internal one. Mysticism he regards as the "mirror picture" of realism and finds that both realism and mysticism, starting from different poles, arrive at nothingness as the object of knowledge. But, says Royce, the realist does not intend this result, whereas the mystic seems to glory in the fact and therefore must regard this conclusion as an indictment of logic and language rather than a disappointment of aim. In comparison with realism, Royce finds mysticism to be a much more self-critical way of knowing. The mystics' paradoxes are quite conscious devices, and their self-critical, dialectical method Royce positively admires. Royce also admires an interpretation of reason which he identified in his study of Meister Eckhart. Reason is held to have its source and ground in a realm (Eckhart's "Godhead") that transcends ordinary reasoning (of subject-object antithesis) and displays its limits.

But a main problem with mysticism, in Royce's analysis, is that it tends to deny altogether the worth of finite life and finite ideas. When mystics say that God (the Absolute) is Nothing and also say that the finite pathway to God is nothing, they lose the "contrast" that the mystics usually propose between this world and God's transcendent world. If God is Nothing, as the rejection of all predication of him would indicate, then where is the contrast the mystics stress between this world with its "mere" ideas and the Infinite God?[4]

If, then, mysticism, by its paradoxes, denies the applicability to God of every finite idea, then the idea and the idea's real object (God) are made as independent of each other as the realist makes them. Thus, both mysticism and realism, starting from opposite ends, land in the same place with nothing as the object of knowledge.

The third conception of being, called critical rationalism, is a "philosophy as-if," a kind of proto-pragmatism beginning to be visible in Kant and as *Philosophie Als Ob* specifically represented in Hans Vaihinger.[5]

---

[4] Ibid., p. 181.

[5] Gabriel Marcel indicates that Royce may have had Vaihinger in mind in criticizing this view. In *The Spirit of Modern Philosophy* and *The Problem of Christianity* Royce had mentioned Vaihinger's article, "Zu Kant's Widerlegung des Idealismus." Gabriel Marcel, *Royce's Metaphysics*, trans. Virginia and Gordon Ringer (Westport: Greenwood Press, 1975), p. 16. Bruce Kuklick thinks that Royce had James in mind. Royce's argument in *The World and the Individual* against critical rationalism is the same as arguments against James propounded by Royce elsewhere. Bruce Kuklick, *Josiah Royce: An Intellectual Biography* (Indianapolis: The Bobbs-Merrill Co., Inc., 1972), p. 253, n. 23. Chapter 6, "Absolute Pragmatism," pp. 119–135, is very instructive as is Kuklick's book as a whole. No theoretical difference would hinge on whether the representative of critical rationalism should be Vaihinger or James. Either could be taken as representing the view. It could be of possible historical interest to know that Royce's analysis of (and appropriation of some elements in) pragmatism is not merely reactive to James himself but very likely goes back to Royce's study of post-Kantians.

Critical rationalism seems to Royce to offer an improvement on realism, and in his own theory of ideas, he goes a long way toward adopting some of its premises. Critical rationalism is an empiricism that takes a pragmatic, prospective stance. It assumes that the knower has some experience of facts which for their validation must point "to further possible experience."[6] It is this prospective fulfillment of the original experience in a later possible one that, for critical rationalism, warrants the assertion of being. So far, Royce can be favorably disposed toward this view and even its empiricism. He agrees that validity is to be tested by experience (to his mind, eventually the experience of Absolute Consciousness).

Royce's chief criticism of critical rationalism lies in what he regards as the nebulous notion of "possible" experience. Royce is very clear in asserting that whatever is a real experience must be some individual's actual experience, and the generalized notion, possible experience, is not itself any finite individual's actual experience. What and where is it? It seems to lie in a merely ideal world unrelated to actual experience. Like realism and mysticism, then, critical rationalism fails to provide the necessary linkage, but here the gap to be bridged is not that between idea and object but between the finite individual's actual experience and an idealized, possible experience not grounded in actuality.

Critical rationalism seems to Royce to be an unstable theory. It breaks either into realism or idealism, and Royce thinks that it ought to break into his own kind of idealism. Merely possible experience ought to become the actual experience of Absolute Consciousness. Such an Absolute Consciousness is required because all the relations (cause, degree, etc.) on which the unity and continuity of our common experience and of scientific inquiry depend are not *as a whole* ever actually experienced by the finite individual. What is required is a "Universal Consciousness in which exists the physical world and the individual consciousness of the particular thinker."[7]

In Royce's own metaphysical view, which he calls simply the "Fourth Conception of Being," he will argue that it is a self-contradiction to reject this Absolute Consciousness, which alone can make our finite experience coherent and real, and which alone can bridge the gap between our idea of an object and the object itself. A common feature in Royce's criticisms of the other three metaphysical views is that they do not provide "real linkages" between the knower and the reality known.[8] So Royce's task is to set about correcting this failure.

One way he provides for a linkage is to invest the idea with meaning,

[6] Royce, *The World and the Individual*, Vol. 1, p. 245.

[7] Josiah Royce, *The Religious Aspect of Philosophy* (New York: Harper Torchbook, 1958), p. 371.

[8] Royce, *The World and the Individual*, Vol. 1, p. 127; Vol. 2, Chap. 2, "The Linkage of Facts," pp. 45–107.

intention, or will. For Royce, "an Idea is any state of mind that has a conscious meaning." "A brute noise, merely heard, is no idea." But any state or complex state of mind that expresses a purpose that I have is an idea. What Royce calls the "internal meaning" of an idea is its capacity to express (or Royce says "embody") my purpose. The external meaning of an idea is that idea's meaning further expressed in the world of "outer facts."[9] For example, my wish (intention) to express my feeling of affection becomes "embodied" first in the *idea* of my friend. So far we have the idea's "internal meaning." It is a movement between my own intention and the idea I entertain on account of my intention. Then suppose that I meet the very friend of whom, with the use of my idea, I am thinking. The actual bodily presence of the friend (the external object) is the further fulfillment of the idea's intention and represents the "external meaning" of my idea. Royce thinks that the best way to put the question of the linkage between an idea and its object is not (as with realism) through some matching of idea with the object which "causes" the idea—an impossible task. The linkage should be understood in terms of intention and the experience of having that intention fulfilled in actual experience.

In terms of this analysis, the realist position tends to separate internal and external meaning (subjective intention from objective fact) so that they only "meet as foreign powers."[10] The realist is interested only in external meaning. Royce has us consider how a realist would view the situation of someone standing at the shoreline and counting the ships within view out at sea. From the realist's perspective no purpose of mine will in any way affect the number of real ships that are really there. When I count them, the realist judges that a right or wrong count is wholly determined by the external facts (or "external meaning"). The realist entirely separates external meaning from internal meaning and labels the latter "mere ideas." Any personal interest, to the realist, is a distorting influence and mere subjectivity.

But Royce points out the role played by the intentionality of ideas:

> The counting of ships is valid or invalid *not* alone because of the supposed independent being of the ships, but also because of the conscious act whereby just this collection of ships was first consciously selected for counting. After all, then, no idea is true or is false except with reference to the object that this very idea first means to select as its own object. Apart from what the idea itself thus somehow assigns as its own task, even that independent being yonder . . . cannot determine the success or failure of the idea. It is the idea then that first says: 'I mean this or that object. That is for my object. Of that I am thinking. To that I want to conform.'[11]

9 Ibid., Vol. 1, pp. 24, 26.
10 Ibid., p. 35.
11 Ibid., p. 31.

So, says Royce, unless ideas "voluntarily bind themselves to a given task" and "commit themselves to a certain selection of its object, they are neither true nor false."[12] We can see something of James's theory of ideas here.

What turns out to be the correct count of ships or the true or the real, then, has to do with the success or fulfillment of an idea's intention in *actual* experience. When pushed to its logical conclusion, that experience cannot be entirely limited to the finite individual's experience because a more universal *actual* experience than is fully available to the finite individual is necessary to account for an orderly, unified world as to which there can be such a thing as truth or its contradiction, error. That there must be such a distinction between truth and error, Royce argues very forcefully. Without it there is the mere hypothesis, the merely possible in which there can be no assertion of being at all. In the examples Royce chooses in propounding this argument, the impression is inescapable that he has James in mind.

Whatever is, Royce holds, must be "continuously known" and therefore "present to the insight of a single Self-conscious Knower, whose life includes all that he knows, whose meaning is wholly fulfilled in his facts, and whose self-consciousness is complete."[13] Royce thinks that this assertion can be defended on the grounds that its denial can be shown to be self-contradictory. "Whoever denies this conception covertly, so we affirm, asserts it whenever, expressly or by implication, he talks of Being at all. For to talk of Being is to speak of fact that is either present to a consciousness or else nothing."[14]

By way of illustration, Royce brings forward just such a skeptic who doubts that beyond one's fragmentary consciousness there is anything at all. Made into an assertion, the skeptic's position holds that "a certain finite momentary collection of empirical facts, ideas, desires, etc., merely called the present moment, is the universe."[15]

Now we are to label this collection of the present moment "A." If the skeptic really asserts that only A is real, then the skeptic has also supposed some direct experience of the whole universe of being and claims to find in it nothing but A. Thus, on the skeptic's premises, ontological predication cannot, without self-contradiction, be made as to the whole of things.

Royce thought that his fourth conception of being had in it many of the

---

[12] Ibid., p. 32.

[13] James felt pushed by this sort of argument for the necessity of continuity, and in his doctrine of "radical empiricism" he tried to account for the necessary continuity in relations by making relations themselves, and not merely separate objects only, a part of experience. An "overlap" between segments of experience is held to be enough to account for the needed continuity without recourse to the Absolute Consciousness. See James's essay, "The Meaning of Truth" and John Morrison Moore, *Theories of Religious Experience* (New York: Round Table Press, 1939), p. 20.

[14] Royce, *The World and the Individual*, Vol. 1, p. 400.

[15] Ibid., p. 371.

positive ideas offered in the other three theories and none of their chief disadvantage, the absence of linkage between knower and known. The fourth conception would agree with mysticism that "in so far as identifying Being with fulfillment of purpose, the mystic says of the object of any of your ideas: *That art Thou.*"[16] But the fourth conception differs from mysticism when mysticism resorts wholly to negation and to every single finite idea declares, "Neti, Neti." We return, then, to consider more closely Royce's analysis of mysticism.

Royce on Meister Eckhart and Mysticism

Prior to the Gifford Lectures, Royce had studied Meister Eckhart, the medieval German mystic, and presented a paper at the Plymouth School of Ethics in 1894. This essay is published for the first time in 1898 in the collection *Studies of Good and Evil.* As we have seen, Royce thinks that mysticism deserves to be criticized if it negates absolutely all finite efforts and thereby devalues the worth of life here and now. But mysticism is to be admired for being self-critical. Royce regards Meister Eckhart as the special example of this sort of self-criticism as applied to reason.

Eckhart's idea of transcended reason seems especially significant to Royce. It means that reason is not merely held to stop short so that (as Royce puts it) the "accident" of revelation comes to fill it out where it meets an obstacle. (Royce implies that Thomas Aquinas has this accidental, filled-out view of revelation.) Eckhart's notion is rather that even the complete knowledge of God "just because of its completeness, would see its own very self as essentially rooted in a certain central mystery." Thus the mystery at the core of reality is not a "mischance of our human reason. It is the very nature of all reason."[17]

Taking suggestions from Eckhart, Royce distinguishes two ways of regarding the unknowable: the agnostic's "trivial" way and the mystic's more profound way. The agnostic way of characterizing the unknowable is the position roughly similar to that of the realist conception of truth. On one side is the world of real objects. Over against that is the knower, the sentient, rational person who can know only by interpreting incoming sense-data. But things-in-themselves have no sense data; so the knower cannot ever get to reality itself and is left with a blank unknown. The agnostic (such as Herbert Spencer) simply acknowledges this defeat.

Royce thinks that we get important clues from Eckhart on a better way than that of the realist to understand truth and mystery. Eckhart allows us to see that God's life itself (Godhead, *Essentia,* Oneness) is beyond all distinc-

---

[16] Ibid., p. 355.
[17] Josiah Royce, "Meister Eckhart," in *Studies of Good and Evil* (Hamden: Archon Books, 1964), p. 269.

tion. Therefore "it can itself never enter into the world of knowledge, for that world is derived from it." The mystery of God is not like a momentary, frustrating barrier to knowledge; it is a mystery that is essentially and logically unfathomable. "You are limited by unknown objects within the world of conceivable knowledge. But the source of the very world of knowledge is itself no object in that world." If, then, by truth one means an object of knowledge, then the Godhead, as the source of the truth, is never to be described as a part of the world of truth, "which at best is the result and not the inclusive container of God's essence." Therefore, says Royce, whoever wishes to seek God and to follow the journey to its absolute end "must first lay aside the very conditions of knowledge, and pass into the still wilderness where there is no longer subject or object."[18]

When Royce moves on to consider the practical, rather than the strictly metaphysical, implications of mysticism as found in Eckhart he points out two practical advantages: courage and certainty. One who "has faced once and for all the central issue of life" is able to be fearless when facing lesser issues and sorrows. And the one who has "in a measure transcended even the dogma of his infallible Church, is not likely to speak with an uncertain sound."[19] Later we shall find that Hocking has a similar insight and finds mysticism to be a motivating factor in activist, worldly reform.

Mysticism does have its practical shortcomings. Royce regards quietism, an "often fairly pathological tendency towards dreamily passive emotions," to be one of them. This flaw in mysticism is a consistent complaint of Royce. In his own brand of idealism he would give deeds and rational thinking a much more positive valuation in the total scheme of things. "If the highest union with God means an absorption in the presence of this mystery—well, then, is not the best, even in this life, a deedlessly passive and unspeakable rapture in God, a doing of nothing, a fascinated gazing towards the exalted Essence, which is to ordinary thought a mere Nothing, but to the mystic is All?"[20]

But, according to Royce, Meister Eckhart does not fall into this quietistic error "except in consciously hyperbolic speech." In Royce's interpretation of Eckhart, the soul, in union, is never so fully absorbed as to lose individuality altogether. There remains a mark of personal identity called by Eckhart the "Punctlein" by which (to follow Royce's quotation of Eckhart) "it returns again into itself, and knows itself to be a creature."[21] Royce takes this conception to indicate a fundamental difference between Eckhart's mysticism and that of the Hindu "That art Thou" dismissal of individuality.

It is not possible to say whether Royce's interpretation of Eckhart is in every detail correct. Probably it is not. In any case, it is Royce's own view of

[18] Ibid., pp. 276, 277, 283.
[19] Ibid., pp. 287, 285.
[20] Ibid., p. 287.
[21] Ibid., pp. 289, 290 (Royce quoting Eckhart).

mysticism by means of Eckhart that we are concerned with here. It is plain that Royce interprets Eckhart so as to minimize any nihilism or quietism that inhabits his doctrine. Union or surrender to God Royce wants to find—and he thinks Eckhart finds—"as much a positive as a negative process." The nineteenth-century morally strenuous life is what Royce advocates and, as a matter of fact, seems to find Eckhart advocating. Eckhart's perspective, in Royce's interpretation, is a coping with life rather than a withdrawal from it. It is "no quietism, but endless activity, even strife."[22]

From our whole review of Royce, we can see that he regards mysticism as a theory of being that he finds suggestive but untenable. His argument against it is based on his criticism of realism because he thinks of mysticism as an interior, spiritual kind of realism. Royce's analysis of mysticism, although critical, can be exceedingly sympathetic and penetrating. A number of issues emerge that students of mysticism would find fruitful for further reflection.

First, in his study of Eckhart, Royce identifies two dialectically related moral aims. Mysticism can offer a transcendent perspective by which to take a courageous risk and to suffer a sorrow without being defeated. Mysticism can engender courage and even activism in behalf of an idea. On the other hand, mysticism is also quietistic and subject to "dreamily passive emotions."[23] Paradoxically, the mystics' other-worldly perspective yields both of these possibilities. Hocking will make a special doctrine out of these two perspectives and their dialectical relation. Hocking does not derive these ideas from Royce, but he develops them into a practical principle called "the principle of alternation." We do not need to choose only one of these alternatives. We can have them both, so Hocking's principle of alternation holds, but we can have them, under the conditions of finitude, only in alternation.

Another theme that emerges in Royce's analysis of mysticism is the idea of immediacy as an attained immediacy. Certainly in Royce's view, the mystic is a person who tries to get to reality by means of experience and that experience is immediate. It may be "immediate," however, in the special meaning of the word employed by Royce in some of his discussion of mysticism. Royce says that "mysticism consists in asserting that to be means, simply and wholly, to be immediate as what we call pure color, pure sound, pure emotion, are already in us partly and imperfectly immediate."[24]

The words "partly" and "imperfectly" are significant modifiers because Royce holds immediacy to be of two kinds. There is the immediacy of "brute fact," an immediacy of sensed data that provides only the "raw material" of meaning. And there is another, a final, fulfilled, purer, perfected immediacy

---

[22] Ibid., pp. 292, 294.
[23] Ibid., p. 287.
[24] Royce, *The World and the Individual*, Vol. 1, p. 80.

that represents the end of the mystic's quest, where thought is "quenched" because it is fulfilled. Thus mere sensory immediacy, the imperfected immediacy of brute fact, comes at the beginning instead of in an attained vision of unity. As an empiricist, then, the mystic does not think of the Absolute as an experienced entity in the same way that the realist would think of an object like "money," for example, as a real, immediately given object. Nevertheless, Royce does hold that mystics are empiricists in their special way. "Indeed, I should maintain that mystics are the only thoroughgoing empiricists in the history of Philosophy."[25]

Modern idealists like Royce, Hocking, and John Caird could understand this attained immediacy in an Hegelian framework by which "progress" is not an overcoming of a temporal or spatial separation. John Caird, who is quoted extensively by both James and Royce as an example of Hegelian idealism, speaks as follows: "Oneness of mind and will with the divine mind and will is not the future hope and aim of religion but its very beginning and birth in the soul. . . . The religious life is progressive; but religious progress is not progress *towards*, but *within* the sphere of the Infinite."[26] We will see later that Hocking defines religion itself as "anticipated attainment." Then we will have to ask of him how we are to understand a spiritual progress interpreted as a (to quote Hocking) "growing acquaintance, adding ideas which from the first have been true within their own intention."[27]

A third issue, the role of reason and paradox, especially interested Royce and has already been mentioned in the discussion of Eckhart. A frequently noted characteristic of mysticism is that radical criticism of ordinary reasoning processes that it represents. Using a favorite word, Royce repeatedly describes the mystic's quest as a "quenching" of reason and thought. As a theory he says mysticism holds that "to be real means to be in such wise Immediate that, in the presence of this immediacy, all thought and all ideas, absolutely satisfied, are quenched, so that the finite search ceases, and the Other is no longer another, but is absolutely found."[28]

Mysticism is a critic of language and is anti-intellectualist in the sense that mystics do doubt, and doubt systematically, the applicability of concepts to the Absolute. Does that mean that mysticism is irrational? No serious thinker, least of all one as rigorous as Royce, would bother to analyze

---

[25] Ibid., pp. 156, 167, 144, 81.

[26] Quoted and abridged in William James, *Varieties of Religious Experience* (New York: Collier, 1961), p. 353. The quotation can be found in John Caird, *An Introduction to the Philosophy of Religion* (New York: Macmillan and Co., 1881), pp. 296–98. Royce quotes Caird in Appendix C, "The Hegelian Theory of Universals," in *The Spirit of Modern Philosophy* (Boston: Houghton Mifflin Co., 1931), pp. 496–99. For Royce's discussion see specifically *The World and the Individual*, Vol. 2, pp. 297–305.

[27] William Ernest Hocking, *The Meaning of God in Human Experience* (New Haven: Yale University Press, 1912),. p. 323.

[28] Royce, *The World and the Individual*, Vol. 1, pp. 155–56, 144.

mysticism at all if it were simply irrational. The prior question is always, what is the nature of reason? Mysticism, to a large extent, becomes of interest in philosophical discussion because it raises this question and suggests some answers.

For idealists in the Platonist tradition the answer could be found in the Neo-Platonist distinction between *epistēmē* and *nous*, that is, between logical reasoning and rational intuitive vision. God (or the One or the Absolute) could then be held to be accessible to reason as vision even though not wholly explainable or discussable by reasoning. In German idealism the distinction becomes roughly that between *Verstand* (*epistēmē*) and *Vernunft* (*nous* or vision). Emerson and the New England Transcendentalists made a similar distinction in terms of Reason (*nous*) and "mere" Understanding (*epistēmē*). Christian mystics are typically influenced by this sort of Platonist distinction, as was Eckhart.[29]

Royce appreciates Eckhart's understanding of reason as self-critical and self-transcending. God, the Absolute, or, in Eckhart's terms, the Godhead, cannot be known as an object within the subject-object antithesis of the common-sense world. The Absolute must not be held to be an entity that one simply can locate in the world. It is therefore reasonable to be critical of language made for describing such entities. But Royce thinks the negativism of mysticism tends to go too far. If mysticism concludes that finite language is utterly worthless, then mysticism ends, where it does not intend to end, with a literal nothing. The failure of finite efforts ought not to be interpreted as total. "Mysticism," Royce says, "turns upon a recognition of the failure of all thinking to grasp Reality. But this recognition is itself thought's own work."[30]

On most of these points as to the proper role of reason, we will find Hocking agreeing with Royce. The exception is that Hocking will embrace a mystical realism rather than renounce it. Hocking shares Royce's idealism, but Hocking thinks a main weakness of Royce's type of Absolute idealism is that it fails to produce experiential results and comes only to a remote intellectual conclusion that can, in itself, be no object of worship and cannot fulfill the main pragmatic need within religion. Although Hocking agrees with Royce's criticism of mysticism if mysticism is seen only as a metaphysic, a negative theology, he thinks that Royce does not pay enough attention to the experiential side of mysticism that can be of pragmatic service to idealism. Hocking says:

> When Royce writes of mysticism he treats it as one of the four
> leading types of metaphysical system, identified with the doc-

---

[29] See A. D. Lovejoy, *The Reason, the Understanding, and Time* (Baltimore: Johns Hopkins University Press, 1961); and Margaret Lewis Furse, *Mysticism: Window on a World View* (Nashville: Abingdon Press, 1977), pp. 91–112.

[30] Royce, *The World and the Individual*, Vol. 1, pp. 548–49.

trine that reality is pure unity, the negation of all appearances and pluralities, immediate therefore and ineffable. Of this doctrine Royce exhibits the emptiness in wholly conclusive argument: speculative mysticism needs no more refutation, and shall have none here. . . .

But unquestionably we restrict our view of historical mysticism in identifying it with this result: mysticism has been a much broader thing than this type of metaphysics. . . . We cannot then predetermine the meaning and fate of mysticism by identifying it with a doomed metaphysics. We shall judge mysticism first by the mystics, not by the theories of a few: and the agreement of the mystics lies in that fact, prior to doctrine, and wholly coextensive with religion, the practice of union with God in a special act of worship.[31]

It is widely agreed among the modern interpreters of mysticism mentioned in the previous chapter that as a metaphysic, "speculative mysticism" with its negative theology has the defect of rational pessimism that Royce ascribes to it. There is a nihilistic tendency in metaphysical mysticism that can be destructive of thought, language, and moral distinction. There is, however, another strand within mysticism, and that is a practical, experiential aspect represented in the devotional literature of classic mysticism and represented, as well, in the ordinary religious experience of anyone who worships. It is this experiential side of mysticism that Hocking will find philosophically useful. It is this "practical mystic" who "finds the absolute in immediate experience." Hocking rejects a mysticism of the ontological type when it is "world-avoiding" and "zero-worshipping." "I have become persuaded," he says, that besides speculative mysticism, "there is another, even a necessary mysticism" that is the practical mysticism of the one who worships and "which neither denies nor is denied by the results of idealism or the practical works of life, but supplements *both*, and constitutes the essential standpoint of religion." Such a mysticism "may teach idealism the way to worship. . . ."[32]

Of the two major works of Hocking on mysticism, *Types of Philosophy* serves best to say what mysticism is. His earlier, *The Meaning of God in Human Experience*, gives a more complex story of what use mysticism can be to philosophical idealism. Because *Types of Philosophy* seems to be the better starting place for an introduction to mysticism, in the next chapter, we ignore chronological order to provide an exposition of the relevant chapters of that book.

[31] Hocking, *The Meaning of God in Human Experience*, pp. 351–52.
[32] Ibid., pp. xix, xviii.

CHAPTER 4
HOCKING'S INTRODUCTION TO MYSTICISM IN *TYPES OF PHILOSOPHY*

In this chapter, we take a look at the discussion of mysticism found in Hocking's *Types of Philosophy*.[1] Because that text is out of print, we try to accommodate the reader with no access to it by closely following Hocking's description and organization. In this textbook Hocking discusses mysticism as one of the several types of philosophy which he is characterizing for college students. The other types of philosophy are naturalism, pragmatism, intuitionism, dualism, idealism, and realism. It will be obvious, as Hocking's description unfolds, that mysticism as a type of philosophy contains some elements in some of the other types. It has some things in common with intuitionism (which Hocking associated with the ideas of Henri Bergson). In metaphysics it is like idealism in assuming that reality is spiritual, mental, or personal and that it is one. And like philosophical realism, which holds that a person's direct intuitions of an external world can be trusted as common sense leads one to believe, mysticism holds that direct intuitions of spiritual reality can also be trusted.

As a type of philosophy, then, Hocking holds that mysticism ought not to be associated with occultism or a love of mystery for its own sake. It is true, he says, that mysticism asserts that some mystery remains after our best intellectual efforts to reach reality. But the mystics' interest in mystery comes from their inability to express the reality they do *indeed* experience. The mystic is an initiate, "one who has attained a direct vision of reality" which cannot be described. "The mystic," says Hocking, "is silent not because he does not know, but because he cannot explain."[2]

The mystics' way of knowing is that of the intuitionist. They know by some direct means for which words are of no use. As Lao Tzu says, the one who knows docs not speak, and the one who speaks does not know. But mystics are seldom consistent. They hardly ever keep silent, and, typically, they write a great deal about the necessity for silence. They positively like and see some significance in this paradox.

---

[1] This material is contained in Chapters 33, 34, 35, and 36 of *Types of Philosophy* (New York: Charles Scribner's Sons, 1959), pp. 254–76.

[2] Ibid., p. 255.

It is possible to regard mysticism as a type of philosophical world view that asserts a metaphysic, an epistemology, and an ethic. Hocking now describes this mystical type of philosophy:

> We may now form a summary picture of mysticism as a philosophy. It holds:
> a. That reality is One, an absolute unity, as against all atomistic or pluralistic metaphysical doctrines;
> b. That reality is ineffable (indescribable); whence, all the predicates or descriptives which we apply to it are somehow in need of correction,—including the predicates which now follow;
> c. That reality (as we seek it in the world outside of ourselves) is identical with the equally indescribable essence of the human self,—we may find reality, therefore, either by looking without or by looking within, and what we find in either case is the same, not merely alike in kind, but identically the same thing: the extremes coincide;
> d. That it is possible (and vitally important) to reach an intuitive knowledge of, or union with, this absolute One;
> e. That the way to achieve this is by an effort which is primarily moral rather than theoretical.
> In each of these respects, it is evident that mysticism is the precise counterpart of realism. Where the realist affirms a thesis, the mystic affirms that corresponding and completing antithesis. The spirit of this type of metaphysics, in its "mystical" identification of the outer reality and the inner reality, may be seen in this passage from one of the classics of ancient India [the *Chandogya Upanishad*]:
> "'Bring hither a fruit from yonder tree.'—'Here it is, venerable one.'—'What seest thou therein?'—'I see here, venerable one, very small seeds.'—'Divide one of them.'—'It is divided, venerable one.'—'What seest thou therein?'— 'Nothing at all, venerable one.'—Then said he: 'the subtle essence which thou canst not perceive, from that truly has this great tree arisen. Believe me, dear one, that which is this subtle essence—of its being is the universe—that is the Real, that is the Soul,—*that are thou, O Cvetaketu'*."[3]

In its historical development this mystical world view can be traced in China, in the Vedantism of India, and in the mystery religions and allied philosophical movements of the Mediterranean region around the sixth century B.C. The mysteries were cults which surrounded various dying and rising deities—Osiris in Egypt; Adonis in Syria; Demeter, Dionysos, and Orpheus in Greece; Mithra of Persia and Rome. The emphasis of the

[3] Ibid., p. 257.

mystery religions was on an emotionally satisfying, personal religion that featured moral preparation and a sense of personal union with the god. There were, to be sure, elements of superstition and barbarism in these popular cults. But they provided certain values that individuals needed which were no longer provided them by the now fragmented ancient national religions. They provided a way of being religious that was directed to the individual's psychological and moral needs apart from national, racial, gender, or caste identification. The mysteries gave the individual "a direct personal relation with reality in the form of an accessible deity," and they provided a sense of moral stability for present life and the hope of personal immortality in a life to come.

The vitality of the mysteries had the respect of the great philosophers and of the state as well. Athens established the Eleusinian mysteries as a publicly sponsored cult. Plato adopted many of the ideas of the Orphic cult even though he was also critical of Orphism. The early Christian theology represented in Paul's Epistles and John's Gospel are strongly influenced by ideas taken from the mysteries.

In the third century A.D., Plato's disciple, Plotinus, developed some of these mystery themes into a complete philosophical world view that influenced western mysticism enormously for centuries. Neo-Platonism, as the school of Plotinus was called, spread from Alexandria throughout Europe and to parts of the Muslim world. Neo-Platonism influenced the Muslim mystic Al Ghazzali (1058–1111) and the anonymous thinker called Pseudo-Dionysius who, in turn, influenced almost all the Christian mystics from the medieval period onward. Among them are John Scotus Erigena, Bernard of Clairvaux, Meister Eckhart, Tauler, Suso, Teresa, Nicolas of Cusa, Bruno, Silesius, Boehme, Dante, Blake, and Coleridge. Among philosophers, Spinoza and Schelling have a great deal in common with mysticism by virtue of their doctrine that the One, the absolute substance, cannot be described because all descriptions place some limitation on that which cannot be limited.

Mysticism, then, "is evidently often the product of an intensely philosophical spirit discontented with the mere rationality of philosophy, and of an intensely religious spirit discontented with the dogmatic systems of theology in every creed. It is inspired by the insatiable ambition of individual spirits to know reality by direct acquaintance, rather than by rumor or description."[4]

Because mysticism relies for authority on an individual "inner light" rather than primarily on the received tradition, mysticism is always on the verge of heterodoxy. Joan of Arc, Bruno, and Spinoza are some of the individuals who have veered off from orthodoxy. And among social movements Quakerism, Pietism, and the Anabaptist movement have branched off, at least partly through influence of a mystical spirit. Mystics, believing as

[4]Ibid., p. 259.

they do that they have some inward access to reality, can become great independent characters like Mohammed, Buddha, and Saint Francis. But it must also be admitted that the same inner confidence can produce fanatics. Never mind the possibility of fanaticism, says Hocking: "If there had been but one genuine mystic in the course of history . . . there would be, corresponding to that person, a true mysticism which would reward our utmost effort to recognize and distinguish it from its counterfeit."[5]

Theoretical Mysticism

Hocking has told us that mysticism has two aspects, that it is both a theory and a practice. He now describes mysticism as a theory, as a metaphysical monism.

If reality is a pure unity, then any descriptions or definitions will not do for it. Because definitions mark off one unity from some other unity, definitions are of no use to indicate the whole, the absolute unity, the one. To define is to make a special, a particular thing of something that is not a particular but the whole or the Absolute. Thus the great mystics often give a list of predicates and also a list of the negation of these predicates, and they perplex us by saying that neither list applies to the Real as One. They will say that the Real cannot be called great or not-great; cannot be called good or evil; cannot be called mental or nonmental. But about the Real (the One) the mystic is not neutral or indifferent. Three things, says Hocking, need to be observed:

First, while mystics may refrain from calling the Real "good" for fear of limiting it to their own relativistic view of what goodness is, "Good" is nevertheless closer to the truth than "Evil" would be. Plotinus uses the word "the Good" as another way of saying "the One," but by it he means a good that transcends all particular relative goods. Similarly, while an undifferentiated unity cannot be either termed mental or nonmental, most mystics closely identify the Real with the self and make it a mental, a spiritual rather than a material unity and often, in fact, refer to the Real as God.

Second, the mystic does not know, and cannot claim to be able to describe, the *content* of the Real (God). But *that* the Real (God) is, the mystic does know. So mysticism, according to Hocking, is in a position between theism and atheism. The atheist says "There is no God." The theist says, "God exists," and means that a personal deity exists. The mystic says both are right: the God confined to theistic imagination does not exist. But the theist is also right: God is. "Thus the person who cannot accept the theistic deity, and yet cannot believe the negation of atheism may find a secure, if tentative, position in the mystic's 'that.'" The mystic's negations differ from those of the atheist in that the "mystic has something beyond nature to keep

---

[5] Ibid.

thinking about, to gain approximate or symbolic conceptions of, and to live by. The 'that' of God's existence thus operates as what Kant called a 'regulative' idea; one whose meaning was not in any picture we could form, but in what it led us to do."[6]

Third, the mystic, unlike the agnostic, believes that the Real, although indescribable, can be experienced directly. This direct experience or intuition in the Christian tradition is called a "beatific vision." The words of the great mystics—Plato, Plotinus, Bonaventure, Dante, Eckhart—imply that the experience manifests the Real which transcends all ordinary attempts at description. Plotinus says it is as if one went into the holy of holies and had left behind in the temple the statues of the gods.

So the mystics' ineffable experience of the Real as an undifferentiated One is not a matter about which they are spiritually or emotionally or morally neutral. It is a privileged insight that arrives after an effort on their part. That effort Hocking characterizes as primarily practical and moral rather than theoretical. He next describes this practical side of mysticism.

Practical Mysticism

In Plato's *Symposium* and the *Enneads* of Plotinus, we find the mystic's experience of the Real indicated by the analogy to beauty—an experience open to everyone. Anyone's glimpse of beauty can be much more than some "interesting play of form and the superficial qualities of things." A glimpse of beauty can be "an indication that there is within nature a reality akin to ourselves"; it can become "an invitation to realize our inner union with that inner reality."[7]

Such an intuition of the Real comes, however, only when it is prepared for by some disciplinary effort of the will. Hocking says that "with singular agreement" mystics have found this preliminary discipline necessary.

What kind of discipline would it be?

It is a "negative path" (as it is called in the Classical and Christian West, from which Hocking here draws most of his examples). It is a retreat, a "world-flight," a negative path that takes several forms: physical, intellectual, and moral.

As a *physical* discipline, some kind of abstinence might be practiced. In ancient Orphism, for example, the eating of flesh, certain fish, and beans was forbidden. In a more *psychological* or *spiritual* sense there was often the advice to renounce lesser goods—objects of ambition or pleasure—in order to arrive at a higher vision of the most excellent good of all. Distractions of the bodily sense need to be renounced. Too many sights and sounds pull apart one's concentration and prevent the mind from being "gathered into

---

[6] Ibid., p. 262.
[7] Ibid., p. 265.

herself," as Plato says, where it has "as little as possible to do with the body, and has no bodily sense or feeling, but is aspiring after being."[8] Christian mystics call this sort of concentration and renunciation "recollection" or "quiet."

The negative path in its *intellectually* articulated form is a stated renunciation of all conceptual distinctions and divisions as inadequate for the Real as One. Meister Eckhart is a chief example. The concentration, the glimpse of the ineffable One, requires, says Eckhart, "a forgetting and a not-knowing. He must be in a stillness and silence where the ineffable word may be heard. When one knows nothing, it is opened and revealed."[9]

The negative path in its *moral* sense is a denial that any partial good is *the absolute* good. Even a person's virtues must be suspect and seen to be not altogether good. The fact that a virtue can be defined and named shows that it is not yet that elemental, unitary, absolute Good. Hocking quotes the charming and paradoxical Lao Tzu: "Superior virtue is unvirtue: therefore it has virtue. Inferior virtue never loses sight of virtue; therefore it has no virtue. Superior virtue is non-assertion and without pretension. Inferior virtue asserts and makes pretensions."[10]

These various ways of following the negative path, however, are for the purpose of reaching a positive goal. One must be rid of subordinate goods in order to apprehend the absolute good and be rid of the partial in order to apprehend the complete. There can be no willful storming of the heights; the hoped-for, prepared-for vision cannot be demanded. It, strictly speaking, cannot be believed or assented to. It simply comes; it is "realized."

But what happens to practical living in the face of this negative, world-denying path? If mystics have done what they seem to claim—caught sight of the ineffable but Real—why should they wish to descend again to the presumably inferior everyday world? In fact, says Hocking, the great mystics of history also counsel a renunciation of the unitary vision. Yet a this-worldly return enables the one who has had the vision to be gracefully nonchalant about this-worldly successes or defeats or dangers. The returned visionary, in the words of the *Bhagavad-Gita*, will have renounced "all attachment to the fruit of action." Having done so, the enlightened one has got rid of an overload of this-worldly anxieties and is, in fact, freer to take part in action.

Mysticism is not, Hocking insists, wholly a retreat from the world. "Most, perhaps all, of the original moral codes of the world have been propounded by mystics." The key is that successful action always requires "a union of attachment and detachment."[11] One cannot succeed by caring everything about one's success, and one cannot succeed by complete indif-

---

[8] Ibid., p. 266, Hocking quoting Plato's *Phaedro*.
[9] Ibid., p. 267, Hocking quoting Eckhart.
[10] Ibid., p. 268.
[11] Ibid., p. 270.

ference. Only the combined attachment and detachment allows effort to go forward without excessive anxiety about the results. The mystics' set of attitudes and disciplines fit them well to be moral originators and reformers of laws and customs. Reformers are always visionaries like the mystic.

Reformers sense the wrongness of a given state of affairs, but how? They sense it because the status quo is incongruous, they believe, with some inner standard. "That inner standard, we may suppose, is simply the persistent mystical sense of unity with the Real; and conscience is the intuitive recognition that a proposed course of action is, or is not, consistent with that unity."[12]

The mystics' negative path, then, should be understood as a process of renewing their sensitivity of conscience, of allying themselves with a reality deeper than the flow of natural events. And it could very well be that there needs to be from time to time a resensitizing by those deliberate acts of attention which in western mystical tradition is called the "negative path."

Mysticism Examined

How can anyone as visionary as a mystic ever re-enter the normal currents of everyday life? And how can those who (rightly) pay attention to this-worldly affairs attain, for a time, the mystic's vision of the whole, the One?

Hocking's answer to this question lies in what he calls the "law of alternation." It is a practical principle, and, he says, perhaps "the chief of practical principles."[13] It is a principle that points to the impossibility of making a permanent choice between paying attention to the One or paying attention to the Many. Life simply has a necessary alternating rhythm. People must pay attention to the business of everyday; to the world's bundle of facts, objects, and responsibilities; to the Many and to the here and now. Yet if their attention is forever confined to sundry objects and facts and is never lifted to any other plane, the capacity to see any value and meaning to the facts begins to dissipate. There is loss of a freshness of vision and the beginning of fatigue. The capacity to deal with facts and objects needs "recharging." We are familiar with this principle by the experience of re-freshment that comes from alternating work with rest or play or sleep.

The mystic's discipline, the negative path, renews and refreshes in a similar way, because it "involves the breaking of mental habit, release of strained attention in detail, recovery of [the] sense of the whole."[14]

But there is a further point. Contemplation of unity itself exhausts itself, "runs down." "The mystic must turn again to the world and discover it as

12 Ibid., p. 272.
13 Ibid., p. 273.
14 Ibid., p. 274.

having regained its lost fascinations, and himself his lost powers."[15] Anyone who has a vision of the whole comes again to the many of this-world with new insight into the meaning of the many. The mystic regains a realistic ability to "face the facts," with a fresh appreciation of their significance.

One example of this fresh look at this world is scientific observation or the scientific attitude toward this world. In the scientific attitude it seems a moral duty to submit ourselves to the evidence found in experience and to suppress "what one wishes to find in favor of what one does find." The scientific attitude at its best is characterized first by

> *simplicity and open-mindedness,*—freedom from pretence and personal vanity, showing itself in cravings to be different or ingenious or in the haste to gain startling results,—and in the second place a kind of sixth sense about the way Nature works, which can only come from a *love of the thing*. Both of these are moral qualities, and such qualities as the mystic's discipline is particularly fitted to develop.[16]

Another example is the fresh and poetic appreciation of things. There is an innocent new sense of sound and color, an intensifying of sensory experience that mystic temperaments like Blake and Boehme and Francis of Assisi speak of.

And still another example is a new social ability. Friendship has a way of "running down." One needs for friendship the mystic's detachment from self in order to be constructively critical of friends.

So Hocking concludes that the mystic must be a realist who appreciates objects and facts, and that the realist must be a mystic with a vision of the whole. Some alternation between the two should be the normal course of life. "The Real cannot be either the absolute One of the mystic or the absolute Many revealed by realistic analysis."[17] Each grasps a half-truth about the world and supplements and corrects the other.

Having in mind now what Hocking holds mysticism to be, we are ready to consider in the next chapter the kind of empirical philosophical idealism he espouses and why he thought mysticism was important to it. We know that he thought an idealism like Royce's would not quite do. Royce, as we have said, opposed an empirical (intuitional) means of ascertaining metaphysical truth. But, however close to Royce Hocking was in believing in an Absolute that lies above or behind nature and history and in believing in the priority of spirit above matter, Hocking differed from Royce by adopting an intuitionist's—a mystic's—way of knowing.

---

[15] Ibid.
[16] Ibid., pp. 274–75.
[17] Ibid., pp. 275–76.

Hocking says that he became convinced "with the force of an intuition" that "the supposed isolation of minds is an illusion."[18] This conviction was accompanied by another: that there is an essential kinship between the self and the ultimate object of the self's most sought knowledge. The ground or object of our metaphysical quest is Self.

> In this underlying and substantial self I recognized the Absolute of Royce's teaching. But I further recognized it as the object of that mystic experience whose significance James had begun to do justice to. With this identification, a great strand of speculative and religious tradition could be interpreted and saved for human as well as philosophical uses.[19]

So Royce's negative attitude towards mysticism (which Hocking says he nevertheless profoundly interpreted) became to Hocking unnecessary. We shall find, then, that Hocking drew on both James and Royce when he developed his own philosophy of religion in *The Meaning of God in Human Experience*. We consider that work next.

---

[18] William Ernest Hocking, "Some Second Principles," in George P. Adams and William Pepperell Montague (eds.) *Contemporary American Philosophy*, Vol. 1, (New York: Russell & Russell, Inc., 1962, first published 1930), pp. 391–92.

[19] Ibid., pp. 392–93.

CHAPTER 5
HOCKING'S *THE MEANING OF GOD IN HUMAN EXPERIENCE*

In 1912, when Hocking published *The Meaning of God in Human Experience*, a main criticism of Absolute idealism was likely to come from pragmatists like William James. The Absolute, they complained, was an abstraction that failed to "make a difference" in human experience. Hocking's response was to try to demonstrate the pragmatic utility of the Absolute. What difference does it make in human experience? Hocking did not agree that the Absolute could be a mere hypothesis. He rejected James's will to believe, but he did accept what he called a "negative pragmatism" whose slogan is "that which does not work is not true." Pragmatism rightly awakens the philosopher to the need to look for "fruitfulness," and largely what Hocking has in mind is what has popularly been called "relevance." What relevance does the Absolute have for daily life? A theory is somehow false, Hocking holds, "if it makes no difference" or if it "lowers the capacity" of people to meet everyday stress or "diminishes the worth to them of what existence they have. . . ."[1] Idealism's greatest defect in the handling of religion is its tendency to lose the particular, the historical and concrete. It tends to offer a "religion-in-general." As such it is "not organically rooted in passion, fact, and institutional life" and when the pragmatic test comes, it fails.[2]

In preparing his corrective for this pragmatic failure of Absolute idealism, Hocking looks to what would have seemed to many an unlikely resource: mysticism. Mysticism, Hocking claims, has a practical contribution to make to Absolute idealism because mysticism is *deed*.[3] It is the name of

---

[1] William Ernest Hocking, *The Meaning of God in Human Experience* (New Haven: Yale University Press, 1912), p. xiii.
[2] Ibid., p. xii.
[3] Ibid., p. 355.

> Mysticism, then, we shall define not by its doctrine but by its deed, the deed or worship in its fully developed form. Nothing concerns us more than to know what that experience means, and what it may add to our knowledge of God: but we shall not foreclose these questions by taking a finished speculative system into our definition of Mysticism. Mysticism is a way of dealing with God, having cognitive and other fruit, affecting first the mystic's being and then his thinking, affording him thereby answers to prayer which he can distinguish from the results of his own reflection.

that which one does with respect to the Absolute; it is worship. Hocking believed that in a larger sense all human beings are mystics insofar as they have any experience of reality as a *whole*. And he thought everyone of every disposition from infancy up does indeed experience reality as a whole. "The infant's first thoughts are metaphysical," and God, the religious name of the Absolute, does operate within human experience in an identifiable way.[4] All metaphysical questions, Hocking asserts, arise precisely because God is *experienced*. Such a thing as the ontological proof for the existence of God is to him not so much a proof as a report on the experience of God. "The need for metaphysical thought arises (I venture the paradox) *just because God is a matter of experience*, because he works there and is known there in his works."[5] So Hocking begins, as Royce does not, with the assumption of an immediately given and certain *experience* of the Absolute. And this immediate intuition is mystical. Where pragmatism can only achieve hypothesis, mysticism claims to offer certainty. Certainty of a known God is what pragmatism requires, says Hocking, but cannot furnish from its own method.

The Pragmatic Question

In *The Meaning of God in Human Experience* Hocking begins by asking a Jamesian question: What does religion do? What are its fruits? We are right, he thinks, to take this-worldly values seriously and, in some sense, to test things by them. If we did not, we would have to disclaim any continuity of values between this world and the ideal. If we ask about the pragmatic values of religion the answer Hocking gives us is twofold.

If we have in view the whole sweep of history, then the fruits of religion are the *arts*, and by arts he means to include things like morality and the various social sciences. Religion is not one of the arts, but its work is the "perpetual parentage" of the various arts. If, on the other hand, we have in view the individual, then the fruits of religion are that individual's character. "It is as if a man's religion and his personal quality were in large measure interchangeable terms."[6] Here he seems in agreement with James.

As we have seen in Chapter 2, William James had made the list of the effects or "fruits" of religion in a person's character to include: (a) a feeling of living in a wider world than one's own selfish interests; (b) a sense of "friendly continuity" and therefore willing self-surrender to an ideal power; (c) elation, freedom; and (d) a shift of the emotional center toward loving and harmonious affections.

Following James's lead in looking for the empirical effects of religion,

[4] Ibid., p. 215.
[5] Ibid., p. 216.
[6] Ibid., p. 27.

Hocking points to the "difference" religion makes in a person's character. He indicates three traits:[7]

1. The religious soul makes judgments independently "as if by a fresh contact with the truth itself, it were sure of its own justice."[8] The religious character thus has an independence that makes it relatively free of outside influence and public opinion. By virtue of this independence, the religious person, the mystic, the one possessed of what Hocking calls "prophetic consciousness," can look critically on the status quo and see that things need to be changed. The religious person has a vision by reference to which it is possible to recommend and achieve reforms. And Hocking believes that all reforms begin with this mystical "fresh contact with the truth itself."

2. There is another quality, seemingly opposite to the above trait: The religious character is typically obedient to some "necessity." The religious person seems in "partnership" with some invisible source of wisdom and obedient to it. And it is a partnership that, in the attitude of the religious person, seems already in effect. It does not need to be gained by effort.

3. Accordingly, there is in the religious character a paradoxical mixture of two attitudes: What in this world needs yet to be won and struggled for is somehow a present possession to the religious character. This present possession of distant sources of worth and certainty is called "faith" and to Hocking is characteristic of all religion. "Religion is anticipated attainment."[9] Religion takes the paradoxical attitude that what needs to be earned is already a present possession. Religion has in it celebration and not merely struggle. And yet, paradoxically, the individual of religious sensitivity also does struggle even while holding that the goal of this effort is already a present attainment. This paradox of "anticipated attainment" is, according to Hocking, inherent in religious consciousness.

Although Hocking is thus most sympathetic with James's insistence on the pragmatic worth of religion as its proper test, he argues that the test cannot be met by a merely hypothetical God and the "will to believe" which James offers. Hocking's main criticism of James comes in his analysis of feeling.

Feeling

Hocking refuses to go the whole way with James in (as Hocking sees it) identifying religion with feeling and turning theology into psychology or the examination of consciousness. This identification Hocking regards as one of the defects of pragmatism and of Bergson's approach to religion. While

---

[7] Ibid., Chapter 3, "The Traits of Religion in Persons," pp. 27–34.

[8] Ibid., p. 28.

[9] "Anticipated attainment" seems special to religion. The arts of inquiry have only a future possible attainment:

Hocking agrees that there may be a large element of feeling in religion, he thinks it is quite wrong to *identify* religion and feeling. "The advocates of the religion of feeling," he says, "are not mistaken in referring our various religious ideas to a higher authority, which they call feeling: the mistake, as I think, is not observing that *the higher authority is itself still idea.*"[10]

Hocking insists that feelings are at bottom really *ideas*. Feelings have their natural terminus in some purpose, hence in idea. Even feelings of pleasure have the purpose of wanting more of the same. Feeling finds its satisfaction in idea. Thus *idea* is the pragmatic fulfillment of the expectations of feeling. And here, Hocking seems to be correcting James by means of Royce's notion of the will and intention of ideas. Religion cannot be confined to feeling alone, cannot be identified with feeling and must always have an idea content in order to fulfill its pragmatic purpose. "Holding our pragmatic test to religion, requiring of it that it does its work, we will have no religion without theory; we will have no religion without a creed."[11]

God: The Idea That Fulfills Our Pragmatic Needs

What needs do we have that are answered by the presence in our world of an Absolute? Hocking's answer is that more than anything we need some warrant for *optimism*. And for optimism a monistic world view is necessary; the world, he says, must have a "character."

When one asks about the practical worth of the Absolute, one needs to be aware of what needs we are asking it to fulfill. Those like James who find the Absolute useless for *directive* purposes are disappointed because the Absolute does not answer the question they *put*. It is, in fact, usually the case, according to Hocking, that the particular question one seeks to have satisfied by metaphysical inquiry goes unanswered. And one is well advised to consider whether one is asking the right question. In the religious and moral spheres, however, there are some situations in which the seeking of an answer and the finding of it are not only perfectly matched but identical. These are the situations in which the seeking *itself* is the finding. For

---

The attainment in every Art is future, infinitely distant; the attainment of religion is present. Religion indeed involves a present possession in some sort of the very objects which the Arts infinitely seek. Knowledge, for example, is an infinite quest in the order of nature,—and in it there is no absolute certainty but only a growing probability and approximation: but the religious soul knows *now*—and that without losing interest in the slow movement of science. . . .

Religion . . . is the present attainment in a single experience of those objects [knowledge, brotherhood, moral perfection] which in the course of nature are reached only at the end of infinite progression. Religion is anticipated attainment (Ibid., p. 31).

[10] Ibid., p. 63. Hocking's emphasis.
[11] Ibid., p. 73.

example, the person who wills to have a good will already has one. "Salvation is, to seek salvation, for in seeking it, one has already abandoned his mortality and sin." This is the situation which prevails in morality and religion where the question is not of what can be empirically finished but what start can be made. In morality and religion we have "anticipated attainment."[12]

Immediacy, Indistinctness, and Certainty

One of Hocking's main convictions is that the Absolute must be found in human *experience*. Unless God does operate within experience in an identifiable manner, speculation is useless and may be abandoned. Hocking, of course, believes that metaphysical inquiry is useful and that it arises and is engaged in precisely because God is already operative in experience.[13] Hence the beginning of metaphysical questioning is, by "anticipated attainment," the furnishing of its conclusions. Knowledge of God is, therefore, immediate. "No type of inference, however direct and simple, can quite meet our requirement; for that which we must *infer* is one step away from immediate experience."[14] If one looks back to authorities one "is able to recognize and accept his authorities" only by means of "his own knowledge of God. . . ."[15]

Mystery in the knowing of God is not ignorance but a sign of some glimpse beyond the boundary. It says not merely "I know not" but also "it is known." Human nature has, as Hocking believes, *some prior recognition of a positive being* on the other side of limitations.[16] The type of certainty which we would like to have with respect to God we do in fact have, he declares. To deny that our idea of Other Mind is real (to say that it is mere idea) "implies that we have in mind a type of experience in comparison with which we condemn our supposed social experience as merely subjective."[17]

Hocking takes the position "that our first and fundamental social experience is an experience of God."[18] But when we ask where, precisely, in our continuous consciousness we recognize this, the answer is that it is not a *conspicuous* element of our experience because it is continuous. "As permanent knowledge, with which we forever begin, and *with* which we forever think our world, we shall not expect it to be conspicuous."[19] It is present in any sense of stability and certainty we may have and in our sense of self-

[12] Ibid., p. 198.
[13] Ibid., p. 216.
[14] Ibid., p. 249.
[15] Ibid., pp. 229–30.
[16] Ibid., p. 236.
[17] Ibid., p. 274.
[18] Ibid., p. 295.
[19] Ibid.

confidence and assurance that we are not in a hostile world. It is present in our persistent sense of reality of other minds and in objectivity of mind and in empirical openness. It is present in a consciousness of responsibility and dependence, of obligation. It is present in being conscious of my own creativity as derivative, as a matter of docility. In such ways, though indistinctly, I am conscious of my "Absolute Other."[20] It is through the knowledge of God that we have knowledge of other selves, not the other way around.

Proofs of God are thus a clearing up of experience. "The ontological argument in its true form, is a report of experience."[21] We do not move, as in the cosmological argument, from the world as a premise upwards to God as a conclusion that the world implies. "It is because neither my world nor myself can serve as a foundation for thought and action that I must grope for a deeper foundation. And what I learn in this groping is, that my consciousness of those defects will reveal, though in faintest degree, the positive object which is free therefrom."[22] Hocking prefers to state the ontological argument: not "I have an idea of God, therefore God exists"; but rather "I have an idea of God, therefore I have an experience of God."[23]

Hocking advises that while we are not to expect clarity and distinctness in our idea of God, we nevertheless can expect certainty, a certainty that is not inferential but delivered to us in immediate experience. God, he says, "is immediately and permanently known, as the Other Mind which in creating Nature is also creating me. Of this knowledge nothing can despoil us; this knowledge has never been wanting to the self-knowing mind of men."[24]

The Principle of Alternation

One of Hocking's most creative ideas is a psychological principle which is observable in mysticism, the principle of alternation.[25] By virtue of this principle, one observes that it is not psychologically possible to have the

[20] Ibid., p. 296.
[21] Ibid., p. 312.
[22] Ibid., pp. 312–13.
[23] Ibid., pp. 313–14.
[24] Ibid., p. 297.
[25] Hocking attributes the idea to George Herbert Palmer. He quotes Palmer's *Field of Ethics* as follows:

> When attention is turned in one of these directions, it is in some degree withdrawn from the other. I cannot at the same moment be conceiving of God as the only being of worth, and yet of my life—this fragmentary life—as itself a matter of worth. I alternate. . . . (One) requires a certain narrowing of his vision, a certain exclusion of the infinite aspects of his task, in order to perform that task well (Ibid., p. 395).

But to Hocking's mind, it is the mystics who are practiced in this alternation of attention:

"whole idea" (the Absolute, God) *perpetually* in view. When one pays attention to it (as in worship), one must exclude from attention a great many concrete particulars. And when one pays attention to particulars, the whole idea itself drops out of sight. Psychologically we can cure this by *alternating* our attention from the whole to the particulars. Hocking maintains that the classic mystics are expert practitioners of this movement of the attention. And this principle of alternation, he says, is one of the most practical skills they have to teach. It permits us to be this-worldly, paying proper attention to concrete particulars in the systole-moment of our practical lives while in the diastole-moment of worship to glimpse the meaning of the whole. We must have both particulars and whole meaning; but we must recognize that our existence precludes our having them both *at the same time.*

Worship and mystical experience involve the momentarily exclusive occupation of the attention with the object of worship and the momentary exclusion of the world of affairs.[26] But the alternation between worldly interests and the object of worship is normal. Sleeping-waking, work-recreation, hunger-satisfaction—all these are ordinary examples of an alternation in our attention.[27] Hocking regards mystical experience as a normal attainment of a new psychical level and not an exceptional incident. In various degrees and forms the mystical intuition and the alternation that it involves is a "recurrent event in every person's life."[28]

Not only does the principle of alternation mean that we cannot undertake all perspectives at once. It also means that there must be alternation between partial objects and *the whole.* And this is what worship means. The whole, itself, becomes a separate object of pursuit, "taking its turn as if it also were a part, as if it were *another* among the many goods of practical occupation."[29]

Hocking objects to any way of seeing the whole which would make of it simply a brew of particulars, blending all differences into one. The ecumenical spirit should not try to create a religious "composite" entirely free of particularity. If, for example, beauty were made into such a composite, we would then prefer to have "perfumed music, dramatic music, Wagnerian opera, or in German fashion, music with beer, Gemutlichkeit and a fine

---

This, at any rate, is what has impressed me in mysticism: that the turning away from the world in the negative path of worship (together with the mystic experience itself which marks the limit of the upswing) and the turning back again constitute a normal rhythm or alternation which has many analogies, and a vital function in the human mind capable of psychological expression (Ibid., p. 392).

[26] Ibid., pp. 394–95.
[27] Ibid., p. 396.
[28] Ibid., p. 397.
[29] Ibid., p. 405.

outlook."[30] Both God and the world "must be worked in with one another forever: forever they must be pursued in alternation."[31]

In the psychology of our ordinary knowing processes we find an example of this principle of alternation. "For as a process in time, knowing has to play not only from fact to fact, from part to part of experience, but also between all such parts and some condition of the whole."[32] Scientific empirical knowledge proceeds like this. Knowing a person is both to learn about that person at the "periphery" by the things that person does, but it is also a personal knowledge "by all intuitive seizure in intimacy of the unity from which all these plural deeds are derived."[33]

Mystics, then (all those who worship), can recover their "spiritual integrity by bringing the whole down among the parts, and treating it as a thing of time and space like ourselves."[34] The passive hermit chooses one pole, contemplative vision and passivity. The active person chooses another, the zestful life of pursuing some practical end. But there is a better choice, says Hocking, and that is the choice of both in alternation. "For the life of each is that it may lose itself, from time to time in the life of the other."[35]

The Prophetic Consciousness

A main contribution of the mystic is summed up in Hocking's phrase, "the prophetic consciousness." By it he does not mean knowledge of a future happening, but knowledge that this particular act of mine, done at my particular point in history, has an eternal meaning. Whether this assurance is

---

[30] Ibid., p. 406. This conception also has a bearing on ecumenical religion. Any idea of a "world faith," Hocking says, must take into consideration the particularity and local nature of religion as well as its claim to universality. See his earlier work, *Living Religions and a World Faith* (New York: The Macmillan Co., 1940), Lecture 1, "Religion and Religions," pp. 17–62 and Lecture 4, "Is Religious Variety Too Persistent?" pp. 263–269. See also his later work, *The Coming World Civilization* (New York: Harper & Brothers, 1956), Study 5, "Guides of Interaction among Universal Religions," pp. 137–70.

[31] Ibid., p. 407.

[32] Ibid., p. 408.

[33] Ibid., p. 409.

[34] Ibid., p. 412.

It is not knowledge that is relative; it is the temporal act of knowing. It is my momentary position as a being in time and space which determines that at any moment I may see but one side of a shield—and this limitation I cannot overcome. But such knowledge of the whole as I have leads me by alternating my position to repair the defect of my historical knowing. Now knowledge of the whole, such as guides this alternation between relative parts, is also a matter of degree. And insofar as I fail to overcome my relativity at any point, or find myself sinking deeper into it, I am forced to turn away from all parts, and directly seek a whole that will replace them. Thus I alternate between whole and parts and thereby transcend relativities as they make themselves felt" (Ibid., p. 411 n).

[35] Ibid., p. 427.

attainable Hocking cannot say with certainty. What he does say is that its attainment is the necessary condition of a person's happiness. And we will find him, in spite of the usual characterization of mysticism as world-denying, holding just the opposite: that the mystic's perspective provides a way of affirming the ultimate moral significance of deeds done here and now.

To understand what is meant by prophetic consciousness and how it relates to the mystic's intuitions, we are asked first to consider what theoretical conditions account for a person's happiness or unhappiness. Unhappiness Hocking defines (as did Hegel and James) as a divided mind. The unhappy person is one whose attention is not concentrated, one who is distracted. Anyone who cannot wholeheartedly give oneself to one thing, because of distracting, simultaneous demands of everything else, is an unhappy person. Lack of focus, a divided mind, makes a person unhappy. Even the unhappiness of sorrow consists in the division between "a beloved past" and the present circumstances of living on in the absence of that past. Physical pain is painful partly because the mind cannot get free to pay attention to more wholesome things and, against its inclination, must pay attention to the pain.

One piece of evidence that supports the correlation of unhappiness with a divided mind is the common experience of having happiness restored when fragmentation ends and wholeness of view returns. Recreation, art, music, and worship are avenues by which wholeness of vision returns. "Psychologically," says Hocking, "happiness [is] the continuous *undivided* consent of my whole-idea to the experience or activity at hand; and the empirical mark of happiness is concentration or enthusiasm of action."[36] The return of happiness is the restoration of wholeness of view.

But suppose a person gives all attention and effort to the task at hand. That person, in order to be happy, must believe whole-heartedly in the importance of the task. If there is a half-hearted effort, if one hedges and thinks the outcome does not really matter, then the necessary condition for happiness is not met. So Hocking thinks that one of the conditions of happiness is that it be "destroyable by failure." Otherwise, the present task is not worth the whole of one's effort, and one's motivation in the effort is weakened by a kind of shrugging futility—the mark of a divided mind. Yet if one pins all one's hopes on success in the task at hand, if the task does seem to be all important, and if the task should fail, then the doer of the deed is left in the condition of unhappiness. Defeat creates unhappiness by dividing attention between the present (failed) reality and the not-present hoped-for goal deemed worthy of one's whole effort.

There seems to be a dilemma here. If one remains detached from the results of one's action and in effect proposes that nothing really fails or succeeds, then one cannot enter whole-heartedly into the results and cannot be happy. On the other hand, if one risks everything on the effort and if the results should fail, one is left unhappy with a mind divided between the

[36] Ibid., p. 492.

memory of past hopes and the present evidence of moral failure. Hocking rejects the cynical nay-sayer's way of standing aloof and refusing to make a whole-hearted moral effört with its risk of failure. But defeat does seem to create unhappiness—unless, says Hocking (and here he adopts the mystic's paradox), some way can be found to pursue definite ends by combining "an unlimited attachment with an unlimited detachment."[37]

As a cure for the dilemma Hocking will prescribe the attitude summarized in his concept of prophetic consciousness. Before describing that, however, he offers an analysis of three other ways of handling this dilemma: "the game spirit," "modern stoicism" (pragmatism?), and a view he ascribes to Royce, "altruism and vicarious happiness."

The game spirit is understood by anyone who competes and tries to win. The sportsman tries as hard as possible to succeed and then leaves bitterness behind in case of failure and makes the next attempt to win with renewed enthusiasm. Similarly, the experimental scientist must be both attached and detached to results. The experiment proceeds with hopes of success; yet if there is failure, the failure makes possible a recasting of the experiment and renewed hopes for later success. The sportsman and the experimenter must not become so attached to success that they rig the rules to avoid failure. So the game spirit does have some of the needed detached attachment. But Hocking finds the game spirit inappropriate as an attitude taken toward the *whole* of life even though in segments of life it may be appropriate. This gamesman tactic adopts an attitude of "moral irony" toward the whole. "Is this a satisfactory attitude toward history? Is drama, play, a certain duplicity in our enthusiasms, tolerable *on the whole*, as perhaps it may be tolerable in fragments of living?"[38] Hocking does not think so.

By the tactic he calls "modern stoicism" he designates the viewpoint that makes the pursuit of the goal one's aim rather than the reaching of the goal. In this view the priority is the process of getting there and not the actual arriving there. The pursuit of a good end is supposed to be good for our character regardless of the actual outcome.

Hocking does not label this view pragmatism, but his description of it emphasizes ideas he did associate with it: a focus on the pursuit and the absence of an absolute end. At bottom he thinks this is a modern version of the ancient Stoic's counsel to detach oneself from the results. This world and our attempt at moral achievement in it becomes an arena of futile effort and illusion.

A third tactic, "altruism or vicarious happiness," counsels success in the results but adds that that success need not be my own individual success. The patriot, for example, can say "I may fail, but the idea of liberty must conquer."[39] I as an individual participant in history may not be successful in

[37] Ibid., p. 493.
[38] Ibid., p. 494.
[39] Ibid., p. 497.

my own high moral aims; yet I can find my happiness in knowing that history as a whole will succeed. I can console myself that my individual moral deed, though in itself a failure, contributes to that grand success that takes place at the consummation of history. This, says Hocking, is essentially a way of resignation, but it is a way that he admits "has its religious heightening."[40] It is an attitude of "thy will be done," in which the individual identifies individual success with an infinitely larger and higher success. By means of this identification the individual vicariously rises above the uncertainties of an individual failure.

Hocking held that Royce's philosophy (especially in *The World and the Individual* and *Studies in Good and Evil*) was the preeminent expression of this viewpoint. "Our comfort," says Royce, ". . . lies in knowing that in all this life ideals are sought, with incompleteness and with sorrow, but with the assurance of the divine triumph in Eternity lighting up the whole."[41] Thus, according to Royce, if my individual happiness does not happen to be possible under the conditions of my present existence, I do at least have vicarious happiness. What the eternal triumph will be I do not know first hand. That it will be is all, according to Royce, that I can have. Resignation is the attitude his view seems to require.

Now Hocking is not satisfied with this result either. Certainly he holds with Royce that vicariousness and altruism are indeed necessary to happiness. But to settle for happiness and success that come only by vicarious identification with a larger whole takes away the zest for one's own moral task. It is a view that moves the focus from this world to a realm above or beyond this world. Vicarious identification with a larger whole does not provide "an adequate motive for treating this present business as of infinite importance."[42] Essentially it is a view that counsels taking refuge from the world and being passive. My moral task, in this interpretation, is not (as Hocking thinks it should be) to be a reformer of this world. It is, rather, to be resigned to the ongoing process of history which I can only trust will prove successful in the end. Hocking thinks that this tactic—essentially that of Royce—provides only a world-denying result and the attitude of passive resignation: In it "I can never taste the quality of genuine happiness, namely, perfect belief in and devotion to my own undertaking. I am a necessarily diminished and divided being: I am to act but another than I is to succeed."[43]

What, then, does Hocking suggest? He believes that the individual must feel more in possession of power to act than such a view as this provides. By power he does not mean ruthlessness, but a sense of one's own ability to shape particular events toward good ends. The prophetic consciousness is

[40] Ibid., p. 498.
[41] Ibid., p. 499. Hocking quoting Royce.
[42] Ibid., p. 500.
[43] Ibid., pp. 501–02.

this very conviction that the individual has the power to command events, and has the power to succeed in the individual's own segment of history. The prophetic consciousness perceives the connection between the success of one's own individual action and the whole of destiny.

And what is the source of prophetic consciousness? The prophet is one who presumes to make a total present judgment on the world. The courage to do so derives, so Hocking believes, from an intuited relation to the Absolute. "The prophet is but the mystic in control of the forces of history, declaring their necessary outcome: the mystic in action is the prophet."[44] The greatest mystics have been great founders, doers, even agitators. "There are no deeds more permanent than those of the Buddha, of Mohammed, of Jesus."[45]

Hocking's assessment of the resources that lie in mysticism is certainly surprising, in view of the common and often merited criticism that mysticism is escapist and other-worldly. But, in fact, Hocking claims that the mystic's intention is the means through which the individual of religious sensitivity gains a sense of moral responsibility here and now. The will to ask what needs to be done and to do it, the will to confront an adversary, the will to upset the status quo and pursue reforms—these aspects of moral courage depend on a prior assurance that comes only with the mystic's vision. The prophetic consciousness is precisely the mystic's vision turned toward the particulars of history, where it stirs the individual to an indicated moral task having eternal significance.

[44] Ibid., p. 511.
[45] Ibid., p. 512.

CHAPTER 6
EXPERIENCE, DOUBT, AND CERTAINTY:
SOME CRITICAL QUESTIONS

Like many of the modern interpreters of mysticism mentioned in Chapter 2, Hocking took a broadly humanistic (not to imply reductionistic) view of religion. That stance meant that as he examined mysticism he looked for ideas of universal validity and application.

Hocking on Mysticism

Essentially, Hocking sees mysticism as an immediate, social intuition of the Absolute Other, and as such mysticism is open to everyone. He thinks that mysticism is at the heart of all common worship, that to try to do away with mysticism is also to do away with that impulse lying within all religious institutions. Church and mysticism—despite their uneasy alliances in history—stand or fall together. To reject mysticism out of hand, Hocking calls indiscriminate. "It may be one of those things which we can hardly live with, nor yet live without. The effort to dispense with it is the best way to realize its vitality."[1]

So Hocking sees mysticism as the spirit of religion itself. He also finds that it sponsors a metaphysic and an epistemology both of which he thinks are suggestive and useful. The metaphysical theory of mysticism is the same as that of idealistic monism: Reality may seem to be a diversity of things, but it is really only one, spiritual (or social) reality. But because reality is really only one, words will not do to describe it. Words separate, mark off, define. The essential reality, though intuited and known with certainty, is, nevertheless, not fully describable in words.

According to Hocking this ineffable, mystical experience of God (the Absolute Other) is the basic social experience by which human beings are led to ask all their philosophical questions about the world. Hocking thinks that the experience of God is the prior condition and ground of all common social experience; that God is a basic reality on the certainty of which all other discernments depend. But this reality is not known inferentially. God is an

---

[1] William Ernest Hocking, *The Meaning of God in Human Experience* (New Haven: Yale University Press, 1912), p. 358.

immediate, intuitively met reality, evident to anyone with social awareness in everyday life. It is, however, a reality that lacks clarity and definability and which, therefore, cannot be specifically pointed to in any narrow empirical sense.

So among the metaphysical and epistemological assumptions that Hocking accepts from mysticism are: that certainty of God is available within human experience; that God is immediately and not inferentially known; and that lack of clarity (the failure of words) with respect to what is known does not compromise certainty. (We shall have more to say on these and related issues shortly.)

There are also some practical moral principles that Hocking finds useful in mysticism. He maintains that even the world-denying vision of the mystics can be morally useful. It is not useful if world denial becomes a fixed attitude instead of a refreshing alternative moment to busyness and distraction. A main thing that Hocking would have us learn from mysticism is "the principle of alternation." Life has a necessary alternating rhythm. One must pay attention to the present and its varied tasks and distractions. Yet in order to pay attention to present variety, one must have a conviction of its importance, and that conviction can only be had by reference to the Absolute One. Recovery of the sense of the whole is what Hocking credits the mystics with knowing how to teach. And most of them, he says, also advise a return with refreshed vision to the here and now and its multiplicity.

Hocking also ascribes to mysticism the spirit of reform, "the prophetic spirit." For Hocking the prophetic and mystical "contempt" for the world paradoxically means that the prophetic consciousness can be a "force" within the world. It can change things, can make a difference by beginning "*to organize the social world upon its own principle.*"[2] Whoever wants to reform must have a vision of the Absolute Good in terms of which the world's lesser goods are judged. The reformer must be a mystic with a prophetic consciousness that encourages a whole-hearted belief in the moral significance of the project at hand. Such confidence comes only by means of the mystics' paradoxical detached attachment to the world. With it this deed of mine here and now has eternal significance, so the prophetic consciousness avows. The great mystics Hocking characterizes as persons of great deeds. And all reformers, he thinks, are essentially mystics possessed of a prophetic consciousness by means of which they can judge and improve the world. Thus the spirit of the mystics seems to Hocking quite relevant to the practical needs of the world. Like many of the other twentieth-century interpreters of mysticism, Hocking refused to caricature it as an attitude of world-denying withdrawal. Mysticism had relevance for anyone facing everyday moral duties and needing to see how these duties could be significant in terms of a whole.

[2] Ibid., p. 518. Hocking's emphasis.

With this brief review of Hocking's evaluation of mysticism, we are now ready to raise some critical questions about his own mystical epistemology. The title of Hocking's best-known work is *The Meaning of God in Human Experience*. But what is experience and is certainty immediately available within it, as Hocking thinks it is?[3]

Experience

Experience is one of the most ambiguous words in philosophy, and one of the most important for Hocking. God must be a known God, he asserts, known in experience; and experience he defines broadly as the "region of our continuous contact with metaphysical reality." We have to take note of the vagueness of such things as "region," "continuous contact," "metaphysical reality," and even "our." Hocking was content to allow experience its mistiness. His type of philosophy was certainly and intentionally a "wider empiricism," as he termed it. And evaluations of his whole effort will in large part be determined by the validity of a wider empiricism.

To clarify our understanding of what experience is held to be, it is useful to ask three questions of any empiricist: Whose experience is it said to be? What is the content of the experience? And when does the validation of the experience as "true" or "real" occur?

Whose experience is it? Here, clearly, if universal knowledge is aimed for rather than idiosyncratic private experience, the answer had better be "everyone's." And that is Hocking's answer, whether or not his answer is

[3]Questions of what counts as experience and how reliable knowledge proceeds from the interaction of sensation and rational reflection have, of course, been recurring questions from Plato to Hume to Kant to the present. They are not likely to be settled in the pages of this study. We may mention here, however, several studies that have been helpful in suggesting how questions about experience are best stated:

John Dewey, "An Empirical Survey of Empiricisms," in *On Experience, Nature and Freedom* (New York: Bobbs-Merrill, Library of Liberal Arts, 1960), pp. 70–87. This article first appeared in *Studies in the History of Ideas* (New York: Columbia University Press, 1935).

James Alfred Martin, *Empirical Philosophies of Religion* (New York: King's Crown Press, 1945), Chap. 2, pp. 9–28.

W. V. O. Quine, "Two Dogmas of Empiricism," in *From a Logical Point of View: Nine Logico-Philosophical Essays*, 2d ed. (New York: Harper & Row, 1963), pp. 20–46.

John E. Smith, *Themes in American Philosophy* (New York: Harper & Row, 1970), Chaps. 2, 3, 4, pp. 26–79.

Anthony N. Perovich, Jr., "Mysticism and the Philosophy of Science." *Journal of Religion*, Vol. 65, No. 1 (January 1985), pp. 63–82.

John Morrison Moore, *Theories of Religious Experience With Special Reference to James, Otto, and Bergson* (New York: Round Table Press, 1938).

Douglas Clyde Macintosh, *The Problem of Religious Knowledge* (New York: Harper & Brothers, 1940).

Ralph Barton Perry, *Present Philosophical Tendencies* (New York: Longmans, Green and Co., 1929).

Eugene Garrett Bewkes, *The Nature of Religious Experience* (New York: Harper & Brothers, 1937).

persuasive. The knowledge of God available in experience is knowledge that Hocking thinks is available to everyone always. The knowledge of God "has never been wanting to the self-knowing mind of man."[4] It is, of course, highly desirable that whatever one person experiences as real be universally experienceable. Hocking thought that every particular experience had in it a prior social experience of the whole or Other Mind. Thus one does not ever experience a thing in solitude but in "inseparable community with the Other. . . ."[5] He held that if we criticize a given experience and call it solitary and subjective, we can do so only by reference to a real *experience* and not merely by reference to an *idea* that serves as an ideal standard. Thus Hocking finds the deliverance from solipsism to lie in experience itself, and he does not need to work himself out of solipsism by means of Royce's kind of logical argument. For Hocking no experience is merely solitary.

Indistinct Experiential Content

Whether one is persuaded by this, to a large extent, will depend on the acceptability of indistinct notions of the content of experience. Accordingly, a second question to consider is what the content of the experience is held to be.

The history of philosophy suggests a number of answers to this question of content. If we think, in a somewhat fictional but perhaps useful way, of the size or scope of the experience in question, then we are given several options. Some of the smallest units of experience are those of Hume and the British empiricists of the eighteenth century who thought solely in terms of such discrete qualities as sensations of color, warmth, roughness of texture,

---

[4] Hocking, *The Meaning of God in Human Experience*, p. 297.
[5]   When, then, we think of "experience" as something solitary and subjective, we are cutting it off from ourselves, and calling upon the Other Mind to view it so, together with us. Holding it thus, at arm's length, we criticize it, and as we thought, by means of an idea of something better: we criticize our solitary experience by the standard of a conceived social experience which would be more comprehensive. And this idea of a better, we thought, confessed the reality of that better. In truth, we should read the situation the other way. That experience, thus held off at arm's length and criticized is not the Real Experience, judged by standard of an Idea of a better. That criticized experience is but a conceptual part of reality, abstracted from its context, and criticized not by idea (alone) but by the reality itself. The real and the conceptual have changed places. It is through my present inseparable community with the Other that I know that abstracted "experience" to be incomplete (Ibid., p. 281).

See also Gabriel Marcel, "Solipsism Surmounted," in Leroy S. Rouner (ed.), *Philosophy, Religion, and the Coming World Civilization: Essays in Honor of William Ernest Hocking*. (The Hague: Martinus Nijhoff, 1966), p. 23. Compare Josiah Royce, *The Religious Aspect of Philosophy*, Chap. 11, "The Possibility of Error," (Boston: Houghton Mifflin & Co., 1885), pp. 384–435. See Royce's "Fourth Conception of Being" pp. 384–435. See Royce's "Fourth Conception of Being" as we described it above in Chapter 3.

and the like. Thinking of experience in these confetti-like bits meant for Hume that the larger configurations of experience like the self could not properly be called experience at all. As Hocking described it, "Hume had gone out of his house, . . . and looking in at the window was unable to find himself at home."[6]

Certainly a complexity like God cannot be experienced if experience is thought of in this way. If we thought of God as experienceable in this sense of experience, we would be baffled by the absence of a body. There is no point of view which is God's in particular. The social reality that Hocking has in mind is at every point of view and seems to lose specificity and individuality.[7] If, therefore, Hocking is to say that God is experienceable, he must also have a much wider view of the content of experience. He must refuse clarity and distinctness, refuse specificity of empirical validation, in favor of a mistier notion of social intuition.

What, then, are we to make of Hocking's insistence on certainty with respect to such indistinct content? How does it happen that all persons do not acknowledge the experience of God? Can a person with a sure, certain, and immediately self-authenticating experience fail to acknowledge the certainty of the experience? There are such people if there are either atheists or even simple doubters in the world, and there seem to be. Given his premise of certainty, what provision can Hocking make for doubting?

Radical and Preliminary Doubt

Let's first take a look at the radical doubt of atheism. The fact is that in Hocking's way of thinking, a final atheistic doubt is an untenable position. He holds that those who deny the experience of God do so in terms of some other experience by reference to which an idea of God is rejected.[8] Does he really mean, as seems to be implied, that every experience by reference to which an idea of God is rejected is itself still an experience of God? And are there, in that case, really no complete atheists in the world?

Hocking's position does deny all possibility for a final atheistic doubting. He accepts, however, and positively welcomes, a preliminary "atheistic"

---

[6] Hocking, *The Meaning of God*, p. 281. Hume had said "When I enter most intimately into what I call *myself*, I always stumble on some particular perception or other of heat or cold, light or shade, love or hatred, pain or pleasure. I never catch *myself* at any time without a perception, and never can observe anything but the perception." *A Treatise of Human Nature*, bk. 1, pt. 4, sec. 5.

[7] Hocking, *The Meaning of God*, p. 332.

[8] *"The only point of view from which our supposed social experience can be criticized as incomplete is the point of view of social experience itself.* The only ground upon which this idea can be judged a 'mere idea' is the ground of this same idea as *not mere*, namely, as actually bringing me into presence of Mind which is not my own" (Ibid., p. 274).

doubting as a therapeutic corrective for inadequate conceptual thinking about the God who is really and certainly experienced.

Hocking's answer here leads him to a position identical with that of Meister Eckhart, Royce, and Tillich: When God is made into an object, into a part of the world's furniture, then the Absolute Other is made into a something that it must not be held to be.[9] It becomes a finite thing. Any "God" that is less than absolute, infinite, and transcendent is a "God" that must be doubted and even rejected. Doubting and rejecting are, therefore, appropriate responses to anything finite put forward as infinite. Hocking believes that the courage to reject an inadequate idea of God comes from that immediate experience of an Absolute God in comparison with which a finite conception is rejected. All our predicates, he says, are fashioned for a world of objects and finite persons. The Absolute God breaks these categories. If, therefore, we reject some predicate, we do so by way of witnessing to the impoverishment of available language when applied to an experience of God we do really have. Hocking, thus, recognizes a usefulness to doubt and even for a provisional kind of atheism:

> God appears as a being in whom opposite traits are strangely united: but the nature of the Center in which such oppositions agree, or are neutralized, is not picturable—is known, if at all, only to immediate experience. As an object in the world of objects, God is *next to nothing;* so the mystics have always truly said. Hence atheism is truer than many a florid religiosity whose God is but a surfeited agglomerate of laudatory epithets. Atheism is the proper purgative for this kind of religion; and has been historically an indispensable agency in deepening and keeping sound the knowledge of God.[10]

If we ask, then, if a final doubt, an absolute atheism is regarded by Hocking as tenable, the answer is no. Atheism is not finally possible; it is

---

[9] See discussion in Margaret Lewis Furse, *Mysticism: Window on a World View* (Nashville: Abingdon Press, 1977), pp. 108–09. The problem is how to think of God as transcendent and not, as the designation "God" too frequently suggests, as a separate entity, a something or a someone that can be held out and examined. Theologians, therefore, tend to look for ways to designate God without thus reducing transcendence. Eckhart used the designation "Godhead" to mean a transcendent, undifferentiated unity, which he frequently said could not be spoken of at all. Similarly, Tillich adopted such phrases as "God above the God of theism" and "ultimate concern." In their zeal to reject a finite, objectified God, they tend to find it difficult to acknowledge that atheism is really possible. It becomes as difficult for Hocking as it does for Tillich to say that a final atheism is possible. Tillich says that "he who denies God as a matter of ultimate concern affirms God, because he affirms ultimacy in his concern." Paul Tillich, *Dynamics of Faith* (New York: Harper & Row, 1957), p. 46. Hocking's position on atheism seems identical.

[10] Hocking, *The Meaning of God in Human Experience*, p. 323.

only provisionally possible as a corrective. But why, given the immediately certain experience of God, would any corrective ever be needed?

In responding to that question, we consider next, not the atheist's absolute doubt, but the tentative kind of doubt which assumes the need for amending one's idea of God. Is the implied corrigibility of the knowledge of God consistent with immediate certainty?

It is true that Hocking holds that development in religious sensitivity is possible and even the norm. Yet he thinks of it, in the fashion of Hegelian idealism that we noted in Royce and Caird, not as a progress from an initial error to a truth later discovered but rather as a further unfolding of an implicit truth present from the beginning. Such progress, he says, should be read as a "growing acquaintance, adding to ideas which from the first have been true within their own intention."[11] Yet how can a less correct or less clear earlier idea (experience) of God be certain if it is corrected or improved later? And by means of what sort of comparison is the correction made? Any supposed progress in the knowledge of God cannot be gauged in terms of an increase in clarity because God is complex and indistinct even though, as Hocking says, certainly known. Progress cannot be gauged, either, in terms of persuasiveness of arguments in behalf of God's reality because Hocking has foresworn all inferential knowledge in favor of the immediate experience of God he supposes all people to have. He holds that all corrections in one's knowledge of God must still come from one's experience of God. For all ideas of God are experiences of God, and there is "no other court of appeal" by which to correct one's social experience of God than more social experience of God.[12]

We are thus given not so much an answer as a taking refuge in a tautology. But it is not a tautology Hocking falls into unawares; it is one he positively embraces and elevates with the name "anticipated attainment." The nature of all progress in religion, he says, involves immediate attainment, yet one that, paradoxically, must be worked toward. The individual is still left "involved in the unending struggle. We have indeed ceased to respect as religious any state of mind which withdraws the subject from . . . age-long human labor. Whatever may be the nature of that anticipation of all attainment, genuine religion is not inclined—so far as hard work goes—to take advantage of its advantage."[13] He leaves us with the mystics' paradox that those who seek to grow in their religious experience of God make the effort because they already are presently enjoying the fruits of that effort. They seek what thay have already found or else they would not know how to begin to seek.

In answer to the question of whether Hocking can with *logical consis-*

---

[11] Ibid., p. 321. See Chap. 23, "Development of the Knowledge of God," pp. 317–37.
[12] Ibid., pp. 277–79.
[13] Ibid., p. 32.

tency make room for an initial doubt or for growth in the knowledge of God, the answer must be no. But "logical consistency" is the key phrase, and Hocking, in adopting the mystics' paradoxes, is making an attempt to describe what he and mystics generally always hold to be uncapturable by logical consistency: the human experience of the Absolute Other. Hocking's promised immediate certainty, however, seems to raise expectations that his refuge in paradox and tautology appears to deny. He takes the source of the uncertainty to lie, however, with language and not with the indistinct though real content of the experience of God. Atheistic doubt Hocking seems to interpret as a misjudgment as to the capacity of language. Hocking's position is that it is certain that God is universally experienced (known), but that no linguistic description of the experience is adequate. The defect that Hocking attributes to language, atheism attributes to the ostensible reality of God. Hocking, like mystics generally, never takes failure to explain as the absence of certainty in the experience of God. Whether Hocking and the mystics are right depends on one's estimate of the capacity of logic and language to deal with a transcendent reality.

Immediate Noninferential Knowing

When anyone talks of experience or of religious experience, another useful question to ask is, when is it asserted that the experience is validated or verified as in some sense true, real, or authentic? Does the authentication occur in the immediacy of the given experience itself? Or does it occur in some second confirming experience that is specifiable in time and space? Or does the authentication occur over a span of time like the development of new habits or skills or personal character?

William James gives an example of a brakeman in an old-fashioned railway car heated by a stove. While the train was in the station the car filled with smoke from the stove, and when the passengers complained, the brakeman assured them it would stop as soon "as the train starts." When the brakeman was asked how he knew, he replied, "It always does."[14] Experience in this sense denotes an *accumulated wisdom* drawn from the past. Something is learned by rule of thumb and by habit rather than by theoretical understanding. This is the experience of the craftsman, the physician, the soldier—the "experience" of those who know how to do something they have learned over a span of time. Know-how and skill are indicators that one possesses "experience" in the sense of collected memory of past experiences. And this is the basic meaning in classical Greek philosophy, especially as described in Aristotle's *Posterior Analytics*.[15]

---

[14] Quoted in John Dewey, "An Empirical Survey of Empiricism," in *On Experience, Nature and Freedom* (New York: Bobbs-Merrill, Library of Liberal Arts, 1960), p. 74.

[15] "So out of sense-perception comes to be what we call memory, and out of frequently

The Aristotelian notion of the artisan's experience in his craft implied the notion of a time span over which experience was acquired. The experience of James's railroad conductor was similarly acquired over a span of time. Hume and Locke, on the other hand, thought of the immediate experience of the various specific sensations.

James, in the prospective tendency of his thought, projected the validation of an idea into future possible experience (its future "fruits"). In the future one can look back upon and evaluate the hypothesis a posteriori. One can then say, yes, my belief was correct; it is confirmed by the observable difference in the data. Or sometimes James used the example of facing the future and taking a risk in behalf of a belief, the confirmation of which would both come later and also begin to happen now: Belief in my ability to leap from one precipice to another actually enables me to do so and confirms my belief that I can. In James's prospective, "will to believe" aspect, the truth is attained and even identified with the whole process of empirical verification, a process that takes place over a span of time.

In the other tendency of James's thought, that of immediatism, reality is understood as a stream of experience, and it becomes inaccessible to conceptual handling. Feeling now takes precedence over the "logic-chopping," as James put it, of thinking and careful validating procedures.

Hocking does not agree either with the "will to believe" that is the concomitant of the prospective tendency in James or with an immediatism that suggests a nonrational plunge into pure feeling. Hocking's immediacy is that of an immediate social reality, an Other. The reality is not merely the natural object itself (as in a natural realism). It is an immediately given social environment (God) within which natural objects are rightly seen to be "objective," which is to say known and shared by other minds. Hocking's empiricism he calls a "social realism" as distinguished from a "natural realism." As such it largely escapes Royce's criticism that realism cannot provide a "linkage" between knower and a known objective world. The linkage is provided in Hocking in the immediate act of knowing because the content of knowledge is not a separate object but already a social reality:

> I do not first know my physical world as a world of *objects* and then as a world of *shared* objects: it is through a prior recognition of the presence of Other Mind that my physical experience acquires objectivity at all. The objectivity of Nature is its community, not two facts but one: but the *whole* truth of this one fact (which whole I do not see unless I note what I am thinking *with*)—the whole of this fact is community.[16]

---

repeated memories of the same thing develops experience; for a number of memories constitute a single experience. From experience again . . . originate the skill of the craftsman and the knowledge of the man of science. . . ." Posterior Analytics, bk. 2, chap. 19, Richard McKeon, *Basic Works of Aristotle* (New York: Random House, 1941), p. 185.

[16] Hocking, *The Meaning of God in Human Experience*, pp. 288–89.

For Royce the knowledge of God comes at the outcome of a careful
logical process of discursive thinking. Hocking does not fault Royce so much
for the conclusion he arrives at as he does for his way of arriving, only
eventually:

> Upon this way of reaching the Other Mind, we must make
> the following comment. That we are still left with only an
> inference of that Other; a faith and not a knowledge in experi-
> ence. Even though we say, with Royce, that reality is nothing
> else than response (or fulfilling of meaning), we have not so far
> as this criterion goes, found that reality personal save by
> probability of high order. We can still speak only of "the source
> of our belief in the reality of our fellow men," not of an
> experience of that reality itself. . . . No type of inference,
> however direct and simple, can quite meet our requirement;
> for that which we must *infer* is one step away from immediate
> experience. [17]

It is certainly this insistence on the immediacy of the knowledge of God
that makes Hocking a philosophical mystic. And it opens him to the per-
plexed criticism to which all mystical knowledge is subject.

On the one hand, immediate knowledge is the best sort of knowledge to
have. It depends on no other sources of knowledge, whether these be logical
processes as with Royce or experiential effects as with James. Immediate
knowledge produces its own authentication and needs no validation by
something else.

On the other hand, if the skeptic should ask the mystics to produce some
test, some criterion, or some procedure, whether logical or experimental, *by
which* their knowledge could be validated, they can produce none. There is
no mediate "by which" to validate their direct knowledge. Mystics have an
epistemological advantage but an eristic disadvantage. They *know* but they
cannot tell us *how* they know; they have foresworn all *means*, including the
means of telling. As Hocking puts it, "The mystic is silent not because he

---

> We err in assuming to explain knowing by a *dyadic* relation between subject
> and object (say S:O). This explanation bears its own condemnation on its face;
> for if knowing were of the form S:O, S (in every act of knowing) would remain
> unknown, and the relation S:O must be unknown likewise. If knowledge is to
> be *explained*, that is, put in terms of something else than knowledge, our dyad
> must broaden out . . . into a triad (Ibid., p. 252 n).

See how Royce requires a similar triad—logically arrived at rather than socially intuited—in
his much quoted example of "John" and "Thomas." Josiah Royce, *The Religious Aspect of
Philosophy* (New York: Harper Torchbooks, 1958), Chap. 11, "The Possibility of Error," pp. 384–
435.

[17] Hocking, *The Meaning of God in Human Experience*, pp. 249–50.

does not know, but because he cannot explain."[18] So with Hocking. He might well be criticized on the ground that he does not *explain;* he rather asserts and illustrates. But then no *immediate* knower *can* explain or defend or even intend to do so.

In this connection, it is especially difficult to know how to evaluate Hocking's "negative pragmatism," the notion that any idea that does not aid us is false.[19] Does admitting this much pragmatism make up for the eristic disadvantage of self-authentication? Or does it, rather, give away the advantage of self-authentication by admitting the need for an empirical verification that lies outside the self-authenticating experience? If Hocking means, as he says at the beginning of *The Meaning of God in Human Experience,* that some test of immediate experience has a place, has he not then given away the chief advantage of immediate authenticity (the same advantage sought by Anselm in the ontological proof), that of needing no support from any piece of evidence beyond itself? If so, he seems to answer the question of when the knowledge of God comes by answering like a pragmatist, that is, "a posteriori, after certain experimental tests have been conducted." But his usual and, we believe, his most emphasized answer is that of the idealism of a social and mystical realism. Knowledge of God comes in the immediacy of experience, now. Strictly taken, these two answers appear irreconcilable in Hocking.

And yet the best approach to Hocking is to consider the kind of philosophical enterprise he is undertaking. His method is expansive and ruminative. His books are full of suggestive ideas about the larger, woolier questions of life. Hocking's philosophical aim is one that has always been represented in the philosophical temperament: to aid us in attaining wisdom.

There is no reason to think that what is real should only be "clear and distinct" unless we insist on tailoring what is real to suit only a precise process of verification. Clear and distinct things are indeed more easily verified than misty complexities that do not allow us to say "look here and not there." But are not all epistemological methods devised in accordance with some metaphysical assumptions? And should we not, therefore, be sensitive to the particular metaphysic that is being employed when validating tests are proposed?

What Hocking had to say was by way of putting on exhibit at the outset just what metaphysical theory he himself employed. He, Royce, and perhaps all speculative philosophers (including James) write as though elaborating

---

[18] Hocking, *Types of Philosophy,* p. 255.

[19] "If a theory has no consequences, or bad ones; if it makes no difference to men, or else undesirable differences; if it lowers the capacity of men to meet the stress of existence, or diminishes the worth to them of what existence they have; such a theory is somehow false, and we have no peace until it is remedied." Hocking, *The Meaning of God in Human Experience,* p. xiii.

their primary metaphysical convictions, their respective philosophical faiths. The greatest value of such writing lies not in its irresistible cogency but in the possibility that the indicated panorama may be edifying, possibly inspiring, and at least suggestive.

The value of Hocking's type of idealism lies in what it suggests about what attitude and vision to adopt; it is not concerned with what statements might be verified by a strict empirical process.[20] Hocking asks what warrant we have for optimism, and he provides an answer for us to consider as we proceed with the day's business. It is the day's business itself that provides any testing ground needed, and that is a loosely woven empirical test, to be sure. If edification, wisdom, and vision are what is wanted, his is a justifiable method. For why should we confine ourselves to tool-sharpening if while doing so we foreclose the larger, imprecise, but irrepressible questions of life, destiny, and God? And how can such questions be entertained without losing some precision and gaining some tolerance for paradox?

[20] Hocking says that we should be clear about what philosophy proposes to do.

> It does not necessarily insist that every belief must be established by reason. It does not assert that we have no right to believe what we cannot prove. What it does is to inquire what the grounds are on which beliefs are held and *what grounds are good grounds*. It may find a normal place for prejudice distinguishing justifiable from unjustifiable prejudice. It may, in some cases, sanction authority as a ground for belief, aiding us to discriminate between a good authority and a bad one. It may advise us, in other cases, to rely on intuition, offering some way of telling a true intuition from a false one. A large part of its business is to inquire what reason can do and what it cannot do, in the way of supporting belief. This will be a part of our own study. But in any case it holds that we cannot as human beings, remain satisfied with dumb tenacity in holding our beliefs. So long as false beliefs are possible, and such false beliefs in vital matters are perilous luxuries, there can be no virtue in declining to *think* about the foundations of belief. (*Types of Philosophy*, p. 6).

A SELECTED BIBLIOGRAPHY

HOCKING

The two works of Hocking that mainly inform this study of his view of mysticism are: *The Meaning of God in Human Experience* (New Haven: Yale University Press, 1912) and *Types of Philosophy*, 3d ed. (New York: Charles Scribner's Sons, 1959). For Hocking's own advice on what to read from his work on the subject of mysticism, please refer to our note at the conclusion of the preface to this study. A study of Hocking on mysticism has been done in an unpublished dissertation by Roland Rice called "Mysticism in the Philosophy of William Earnest Hocking" (Boston University, 1954). The organization is disappointing.

An exhaustive bibliography for William Ernest Hocking from 1898 to 1964 has been compiled by Richard C. Gilman in Leroy S. Rouner (ed.), *Philosophy, Religion and the Coming World Civilization: Essays in Honor of William Ernest Hocking* The Hague: Martinus Nijhoff, 1966). This book of essays edited by Rouner is a good introduction to Hocking, as is Rouner's own systematic discussion, Leroy S. Rouner, *Within Human Experience: The Philosophy of William Ernest Hocking* (Cambridge: Harvard University Press, 1969). A. R. Luther's study of Hocking, *Existence as Dialectical Tension* (The Hague: Martinus Nijhoff, 1968) is a brief and careful essay on Hocking's social and religious philosophy. The bibliography includes many articles and books by and about Hocking. An excellent and very brief introduction to Hocking is contained in Bruce Kuklick, *The Rise of American Philosophy* (New Haven: Yale University Press, 1977), Part 5, Chap. 25, "Ernest Hocking," pp. 481–95. Hocking is also briefly treated in John E. Smith, *Themes in American Philosophy* (New York: Harper Torchbook, 1970), pp. 153–58 and in James Alfred Martin, *Empirical Philosophies of Religion* (New York: Kings Crown Press, 1945), Chap. 2, "Empirical Idealism," pp. 9–28.

The wide range of Hocking's interests can be seen in a sample of his works. *Human Nature and Its Remaking* (New Haven: Yale University Press, 1918) is a book on social and religious ethics based on lectures delivered at Yale Divinity School. Hocking treated philosophy of law and society in *The Present Status of Law and of Rights* (New Haven: Yale University Press, 1926). Two practical books addressed special topics of the day: *Morale and Its Enemies* (New Haven: Yale University Press, 1918) and *Re-thinking Missions* (New York: Harper and Brothers, 1932). The latter was an evaluation by an interdenominational inspecting committee, the Laymen's Foreign Mission Inquiry, chaired by Hocking.

Hocking's introductory textbook, *Types of Philosophy* (New York: Charles Scribner's Sons, 1929, 1939, and 1959) was designed for an undergraduate course at Harvard and used widely for thirty years. One type of philosophy considered in it is mysticism, and those chapters comprise one of the best philosophical introductions to the subject. Hocking treated the subject of immortality in *Thoughts on Death and Life* (New York: Harper and Brothers, 1937), and in an expansion of that work, entitled *The Meaning of Immortality in Human Experience* (New York: Harper and Brothers, 1957). His *Living Religions and a World Faith* (New York: The Macmillan Co., 1940) is a further reflection on world religions stemming from his earlier world travels in behalf of the commission on missions. It is also a continuation of his idea of prophetic consciousness which he elaborates at the end of his first major work, *The Meaning of God in Human Experience* (New Haven: Yale University Press, 1912). A special edition of this work with contributions from Hocking and John E. Smith was published by the Yale University Press in 1963 but is no longer in print.

Other works are *Science and the Idea of God* (Chapel Hill: University of North Carolina Press, 1944); *Preface to Philosophy: Textbook* (New York: The Macmillan Co., 1946), written with Brand Blanshard, Charles William Hendel, and John Herman Randall; and *Freedom of the Press: A Framework of Principles* (Chicago: University of Chicago Press, 1947). *Experiment in Education* (Chicago: Henry Regnery Co., 1954) is on postwar Germany and the allied occupation. *The Coming World Civilization* (New York: Harper and Brothers, 1956) is a treatment of social philosophy and an estimate of Christianity as one religion among world religions. It continues some of the themes of *Living Religions and a World Faith*. Social and political philosophy is again treated in *The Strength of Men and Nations: A Message to the USA vis à vis the USSR* (New York: Harper and Brothers, 1959).

JAMES

The book of primary interest in the discussion of James on mysticism is William James, *Varieties of Religious Experience* (New York: Collier, 1961). Anthologies on James, from several of which citations have been made in Chapter 2, are: William James, *The Will to Believe and Other Essays in Popular Philosophy* (New York: Dover Publications, Inc., 1956); John K. Roth (ed.), *The Moral Philosophy of William James* (New York: Thomas Y. Crowell, 1969); Bruce Wilshire (ed.), *William James: The Essential Writings* (Albany: State University of New York Press, 1984); and John J. McDermott (ed.), *The Writings of William James* (New York: Modern Library, 1968).

Recent books consulted are: Marcus Peter Ford, *William James's Philosophy: A New Perspective* (Amherst: University of Massachusetts Press, 1982); Bruce Wilshire, *William James and Phenomenology: A Study of "The Princi-*

ples of Psychology" (Bloomington: Indiana University Press, 1968); John Wild, *The Radical Empiricism of William James* (Garden City: Doubleday & Co., Inc., 1969); Morton White, *Science and Sentiment in America* (London: Oxford University Press, 1972), Chap. 8, "William James: Pragmatism and the Whole Man," pp. 170–216, and Chap. 9, "Josiah Royce: Science Christianity and Absolute Idealism," pp. 217–39; James C. S. Wernham, *James's Will-to-Believe Doctrine: A Heretical View* (Kingston-Montreal: McGill-Queen's University Press, 1987).

Older books that are exceedingly helpful are: John Morrison Moore, *Theories of Religious Experience* (New York: Round Table Press, Inc., 1938), Chap. 1, "Experiential Religion in the Thought of William James," pp. 1–74; Ralph Barton Perry, *Present Philosophical Tendencies* (London: Longmans, Green and Co., 1929), Appendix, "The Philosophy of William James," pp. 349–78; Ralph Barton Perry, *Philosophy of the Recent Past: An Outline of European and American Philosophy Since 1860* (New York: Charles Scribner's Sons, 1926).

Works of biographical interest are Gay Wilson Allen, *William James: A Biography* (New York: Viking Press, 1967); and George P. Adams and William Pepperell Montague (eds.), *Contemporary American Philosophy*, Vol. 1 (New York: Russell & Russell, Inc., 1962, first published 1930); and the classic of Ralph Barton Perry, *The Thought and Character of William James*, 2 vols. (Boston: Little, Brown, and Co., 1935). A "briefer version" of this work is published by G. Braziller.

Books on religious experience are listed in n. 3 of Chap. 6. For an indication of James's interest in psychical research see Gardner Murphy and Robert Ballou (eds.), *William James on Psychical Research* (New York: Viking Press, 1960) and Eugene Taylor, *William James on Exceptional Mental States: The 1896 Lowell Lectures* (Amherst: University of Massachusetts Press, 1984).

ROYCE

In this study we have mainly used two books by Royce to discover his view of mysticism. His *Studies of Good and Evil* (Hamden: Archon Books, 1964, first published 1898), contains the important essay, "Meister Eckhart" (pp. 261–97). The other work is Josiah Royce, *The World and the Individual*, 2 vols. (New York: The Macmillan Co., 1923, first published 1899). Royce's criticism of mysticism and his outline of his own "Fourth Conception of Being" is given in Vol. 1. The essential argument for his own view is also given earlier in Josiah Royce, *The Religious Aspect of Philosophy* (New York: Harper Torchbook, 1958, first published 1885), in Chap. 11, "The Possibility of Error," pp. 384–435. Royce said that in later works he never varied from the argument represented in that chapter.

Helpful books on Royce are: John J. McDermott (ed.), *The Basic Writings of Josiah Royce* (University of Chicago Press, 1960) and John K. Roth (ed.), *The Philosophy of Josiah Royce* (New York: Thomas Y. Crowell, 1971). The book on Royce's theory of being to which Hocking contributed the autobiographical preface cited in Chap. 1, n. 1 is Gabriel Marcel, *Royce's Metaphysics*, trans. Virginia and Gordon Ringer (Westport: Greenwood Press, 1975, first published 1956). Helpful studies of Royce are Bruce Kuklick, *Josiah Royce: An Intellectual Biography* (Indianapolis: The Bobbs-Merrill Co., Inc., 1972) and the very recent biography, John Clendenning, *The Life and Thought of Josiah Royce* (Madison: University of Wisconsin Press, 1985). John Clendenning has also published *Letters of Josiah Royce* (University of Chicago Press, 1970). Also helpful is the chapter on Royce in Elizabeth Flower and Murray G. Murphey, *A History of Philosophy in America*, Vol. 2 (New York: Capricorn Books, 1977), Chap. 12, "Josiah Royce," pp. 695–769. For general history and background: Bruce Kuklick, *The Rise of American Philosophy* (New Haven: Yale University Press, 1977), Parts 2 and 3, "The Golden Age at Harvard," pp. 127–402. For biography, personal reminiscence, and selected letters of Hocking and Royce, see Daniel S. Robinson, *Royce and Hocking: American Idealists* (Boston: The Christopher Publishing House, 1968).

INDEX

In this index the association of a topic with either Hocking, James, or Royce is indicated by the initial, (H), (J), or (R) preceding the page number.

A collection of topics on which brief comparisons or parallels of thought have been noted in the text are placed under the single heading, "Hocking, James, and Royce compared on various topics."

The subject of mysticism is shown under the major heading, "Mysticism," and also in separate subheadings under "Hocking," and "James," and "Royce."